Emil Kuichling

Syracuse Water Works

Condemnation proc[eedings] for mills, Mar. 1896. B. R. & P. R. R. case at

Colden, N. Y. Rainfall & runoff on various basins

Emil Kuichling

Syracuse Water Works
Condemnation proc[eedings] for mills, Mar. 1896. B. R. & P. R. R. case at Colden, N. Y. Rainfall & runoff on various basins

ISBN/EAN: 9783337294915

Printed in Europe, USA, Canada, Australia, Japan

Cover: Foto ©Andreas Hilbeck / pixelio.de

More available books at **www.hansebooks.com**

Reduction Factors for Drainage Basins.

1). A depth of 1-inch on 1-square Mile of Drainage Area, is equivalent to a yield (Precipitation or Runoff) of:—

(a)	Volume =	2,323,200 Cub. Ft.	
(b)	Yield =	6,364.93 Cub. Ft. per Day	for one year, 365 days.
(c)	〃 =	9,680.00 〃 〃 〃	240 days.
(d)	〃 =	10,560.00 〃 〃 〃	220 〃
(e)	〃 =	11,616.00 〃 〃 〃	200 〃
(f)	〃 =	0.86738 Cub. Ft. per Second per Month of	31 days.
(g)	〃 =	0.89630 〃 〃 〃	30 〃
(h)	〃 =	0.92720 〃 〃 〃	29 〃
(i)	〃 =	0.96032 〃 〃 〃	28 〃
(j)	〃 =	26.889 Cub. Ft. per Second for	1 day.
(k)	〃 =	0,0736[illegible] 〃 〃 〃	1 year, 365 days.

2). A depth of 1 foot on 1 square Mile of Drainage Area is equivalent to a yield of 0.884016 Cub. Ft. per Second for 1 year, [illegible]

or to a yield of	[illegible]4444... Cub. Ft. per Second for	240 days;
〃 〃 〃	1.46666... 〃 〃 〃	220 〃;
〃 〃 〃	1.61333... 〃 〃 〃	200 〃,
〃 〃 〃	322.666... 〃 〃 〃	1 day.

3). A yield of 1 cubic foot per Second is equivalent to the following Depths in Inches on 1 square Mile of Drainage Area:—

t = 13.5744 Inches for 365 days.		t = 1.1529 Inches for 31 days.
〃 8.9256 〃 〃 240 〃		〃 1.1157 〃 〃 30 〃
〃 8.1818 〃 〃 220 〃		〃 1.0785 〃 〃 29 〃
〃 7.4380 〃 〃 200 〃		〃 1.0413 〃 〃 28 〃
		〃 0.037190 〃 〃 1 〃

Reduction Factors, for Drainage Problems.

Let (q) = Rainfall or Runoff for 1 square Mile in Cub.Ft. per Second;
-"- (t) = Depth of Rainfall or Runoff on Drainage Area in Inches;
-"- (n) = Number of Days in period of Time considered;
-"- (N) = Number of Square Miles in Drainage Area;
-"- (Q) = Mean Monthly Rainfall or Runoff for (N) in Cub.Ft. per Second;

then :—

$$q = \frac{\overline{5280}^2}{86400 \cdot n} \cdot \frac{t}{12} = \frac{242}{9} \cdot \frac{t}{n}, \quad \text{and} \quad t = \frac{9n}{242} \cdot q \;;$$

also :—

$$Q = Nq = \frac{242}{9} \cdot \frac{Nt}{n}, \quad \text{and} \quad t = \frac{9n}{242} \cdot \frac{Q}{N}.$$

We thus obtain :—

No. of Days (n)	For 1 Square Mile (q) Cub.Ft. per Sec.	For N Square Miles (Q) Cub.Ft. per Sec.	Depth in Inches (t)
31	$q = 0.86738 \cdot t$	$Q = 0.86738 \cdot Nt$	$t = 1.1529 \cdot q$
30	" $0.89630 \cdot t$	" $0.89630 \cdot Nt$	" $1.1157 \cdot q$
29	" $0.92720 \cdot t$	" $0.92720 \cdot Nt$	" $1.0785 \cdot q$
28	" $0.96032 \cdot t$	" $0.96032 \cdot Nt$	" $1.0413 \cdot q$

Rainfall Records in Central Counties of State of New York as Compiled in Reports of the Regents of the University of said State

	Station.	County	Period From — To	No. of Years.	Jan.	Feb.	Mar.
1	Onondaga Hollow	Onondaga Co.	1826 – 1844	16	2.52	1.48	1.79
2	Pompey, (1745'+ T.W.)	— " — — " —	1826 – 1843	15 17	1.87	1.30	1.19
3	— " —	— " — — " —	1850 – 1858	9	1.59	2.54	1.85
4	Syracuse (405'+ T.W.)	— " — — " —	1850 – 1852	3	2.64	2.61	2.37
5	— " — — " —	— " — — " —	1843	1	2.46 11.08 2.22	1.83 9.76 1.95	3.63 10.83 2.17
6	Auburn	Cayuga Co.	1827–1849	22	2.50	2.04	2.13
7	Cayuga-Ledyard	— " — — " —	1827–1850	~~24~~	1.93 4.43 2.21	1.60 3.64 1.82	1.64 3.77 1.88
8	Homer (1100'+ T.W.)	Cortland Co.	1850–1863	14	2.80	2.79	2.92
9	Hamilton	Madison Co.	1827–1849	18	2.25	2.65	2.27
10	Oneida Conf. Seminary Cazenovia.	— " —	1830 – 1849	19	2.46 4.71 2.36	2.12 4.77 2.3[illegible]	2.60 4.87 [illegible]
11	Ithaca (440'+ T.W.)	Tompkins Co.	1828–1848	17	1.82	1.64	2.15
12	— " —	— " —	1850 – 1853	4	2.21 4.03 2.01	1.56 3.20 1.60	3.39 5.54 2.77
13.	Seneca Falls (463'+ T.W.)	Seneca Co.	1850 – 1852	3	1.38	2.46	2.91
		Totals of Nos. 1–13, except No. 12			25.63	23.83	27.92
		Means of [illegible]			2.14	1.96	2.33

New York Meteorology." { 1826 to 1850 / 1850 to 1863. } &

Apr.	May	June	July	Aug.	Sept.	Oct.	Nov.	Dec.	Monthly Mean. Ins.
2.02	2.77	3.69	3.41	3.19	2.67	3.26	2.48	1.95	2.02
1.56	2.76	4.38	4.11	3.37	3.09	2.90	1.65	1.24	2.45
3.65	3.51	3.83	3.62	3.77	3.60	4.47	3.50	3.01	
3.26	3.22	4.20	3.53	3.28	3.30	5.26	3.79	3.90	
1.63 12.12 2.42	1.10 13.36 2.67	3.00 19.10 3.82	2.19 16.86 3.37	2.15 15.76 3.15	4.68 17.34 [illegible]	5.41 21.30 4.26	2.83 14.45 2.[illegible]	2.12 12.22 2.44	2.75
2.22	3.45	3.57	3.13	3.23	3.20	3.38	2.85	2.72	2.88
2.09 4.31 2.15	3.73 7.18 [illegible]	3.75 7.32 3.66	3.88 7.01 3.50	3.37 6.60 3.30	3.11 6.31 .16	3.20 6.58 [illegible]	2.03 4.88 2.[illegible]	2.12 4.84 [illegible]	2.76
4.11	4.17	5.47	4.90	3.79	4.00	4.06	3.70	3.23	
1.93	2.93	3.48	3.79	2.70	3.68	3.12	2.54	2.78	2.88
2.78 4.71 2.35	3.16 6.69 [illegible]	4.50 7.98 3.99	4.10 7.89 3.[illegible]	3.58 6.28 3.14	3.55 7.23 3.[illegible]	3.58 6.70 [illegible].35	3.00 5.54 [illegible]	2.77 5.55 [illegible]	3.19
1.84	3.22	3.43	3.35	2.64	3.32	2.56	2.86	1.96	2.57
3.69 5.53 2.76	3.43 6.65 3.33	3.73 7.16 3.58	3.33 6.68 3.34	3.50 6.14 3.07	2.42 5.74 2.87	3.08 5.64 2.82	1.97 4.83 2.42	2.83 4.79 2.39	
3.13	2.84	3.15	3.21	1.98	2.69	3.90	3.66	3.46	
29.80 2.48	36.72 3.06	44.71 3.7[illegible]	41.65 3.47	36.76 3.0[illegible]	39.31 3.28	44.12 [illegible]	38.36 [illegible].78	30.86 2.5[illegible]	

	Station	County.	Period From – To	No. of Years	Jan.	Feb.	Mar.
14	Bridgewater	Oneida Co.	1833-1837	4	4.26	2.84	3.01
15	Hamilton College Clinton –	–"–	1850–1860	11	2.35	2.11	2.60
16	Oneida Inst. of Science &c. Whitestown.	–"–	1834–1841	7	2.74	1.41	1.34
17	Boonville (1681'+ T.W)	–"–	1882	1	–	–	–
18	Utica (510'+ T.W.)	–"–	1851-2-3-4 1860-1-2-3	8	3.90	2.65	3.58
19	–"– –"–	–"–	1826 – 1848	22	2.92 16.17 3.23	2.61 11.62 2.32	2.75 13.28 2.66
20	Canandaigua	Ontario Co.	1829-1838	10	2.94	3.13	2.31
21	Geneva (567'+ T.W.)	–"– –"–	1850–1863	14	2.05	1.56	1.99
22	State Agr. Exp't Station –"–	–"– – –"–	1882–1892	11	1.26 6.25 2.08	1.32 6.01 2.00	1.32 6.62 1.87
23	Oxford (975'+ T.W)	Chenango Co.	1829- 1845	17	2.64	1.98	2.25
24	–"–	–"– –"–	1850 – 1856	7	2.14 4.78 2.34	2.74 4.72 2.36	1.90 4.15 2.07
25	Mexico (396'+ T.W)	Oswego Co.	1837–1849	11	2.27	2.06	2.26
26	–"–	–"–	1850–1862	13	3.56 5.78	3.34 5.40	3.34 5.60
27	Cherry Valley (1300'+ T.W)	Otsego Co.	1827-1845	15	3.13	2.62	2.99
28	–"– – –"–	–"– – –"–	1850–1854	5	0.77	3.19	2.20
29	Cooperstown	–"– – –"–	1854 – 1871	18	2.49	1.73	2.52
30	Hartwick Seminary	–"– – –"–	1826–1850	17	2.66 9.05	2.15 9.69	2.59 10.36
31	Palmyra High School	Wayne Co.	1835	1	1.22 16.05 2.29	0.55 15.94 2.28	1.65 17.55 2.51

4.26	3.47	5.36	4.82	2.74	2.55	4.37	2.12	4.35	3.67	44.02	
4.42	3.78	5.04	4.47	3.76	4.29	4.46	4.23	3.55		45.06	
2.19	2.75	3.39	3.39	2.96	2.54	3.27	2.11	1.96	2.50	30.06	
~~3.00~~	1.02	3.01	3.96	—	—	—	—	—	—	—	
2.43	3.68	3.06	[illegible].36	3.05	3.43	3.43	5.07	2.80		43.44	
3.17 16.47 3.2[illegible]	3.34 17.02 [illegible].40	4.60 21.45 4.29	4.53 23.57 4.[illegible]	3.70 16.21 3.24	3.55 16.36 3.27	2.78 18.31 3.66	3.43 16.96 3.39	3.19 15.85 3.	3.34	40.09 202.67 40.53	203.27 40.65
2.68	4.53	3.89	3.22	3.12	2.81	3.26	2.77	2.36	3.10	37.15	
3.00	2.20	3.54	3.47	3.12	2.75	2.99	2.71	2.64		32.02	
2.00 7.68 2.[illegible]	2.49 9.22 3.0[illegible]	3.83 11.26 [illegible]	3.20 9.89 3.30	3.32 9.56 3.19	2.21 7.77 2.59	2.43 8.68 2.[illegible]	1.98 7.46 2.49	1.25 6.25 2.08		26.61 95.78 [illegible]	95.65 31.88
2.66	3.41	4.08	4.03	2.63	3.25	3.44	2.45	2.25	3.00	36.55	
4.27 6.93 3.47	3.94 7.35 3.6[illegible]	4.4[illegible] 8.54 4.27	3.99 8.02 4.01	3.07 6.14 3.07	4.27 7.52 3.76	2.6[illegible] 6.08 3.04	[illegible] 5.95 2.97	2.92 5.17 2.5[illegible]		40.28 76.33 38.17	75.35 37.67
1.40	2.77	2.38	2.75	2.12	2.79	3.94	3.07	3.09	2.56	33.78	
3.33 4.73	3.35 5.82	3.43 5.81	3.3[illegible] 6.05	3.72 5.84	4.11 6.90	4.03 7.97	3.78 6.85	4.62 7.71		43.56 74.34	[illegible].46
3.09	3.67	4.56	4.41	3.19	3.92	3.64	3.17	2.73	3.43	41.14	
4.01	3.22	2.74	2.25	3.11	1.29	3.78	3.50	5.86		35.92	
3.08	3.82	4.23	4.38	4.58	3.46	3.43	3.21	2.52		39.22	
3.10 12.28	3.35 14.06	4.05 15.58	4.24 15.28	2.91 13.79	3.09 11.76	3.54 14.39	3.20 13.08	2.54 13.65	3.11	37.38 163.66	
[illegible] 22.01 3.14	[illegible] 20.86 [illegible]	5.61 27.00 3.86	4.19 25.52 3.65	4.08 23.71 3.39	3.27 21.93 3.13	5.06 27.42 3.[illegible]	1.96 21.89	0.93 22.29 [illegible]	2.82	33.80 261.80 [illegible].40	33.81 [illegible] 3[illegible].45

No.	Station		County		Period From — To	No. of Years.	Jan.	Feb.	Mar.
1	3 stations		Onondaga Co.		182[illegible] – [illegible]58	46	11.08	9.76	10.83
2	2 — " —		Cayuga	"	1827 – 1850	36	4.43	3.64	3.77
3	1 — " —	(Homer)	Cortland	"	1850 – 1863	14	2.80	2.79	2.92
4	1 — " —	(Ithaca)	Tompkins	"	1828 – 1853	21	4.03	3.20	5.54
5	1 — " —	(Sen. Falls)	Seneca	"	1850 – 1852	3	1.38	2.46	2.91
6	2 — " —		Ontario	— " —	1829 – 1892	35	6.25	6.01	5.62
7	1 — " —	(Palmyra)	Wayne	"	1835	1	1.22	0.85	1.65
8	1 — " —	(Mexico)	Oswego	"	1837 – 1862	24	5.78	5.40	5.60
9	4 — " —		Oneida	"	1826 – 1863	52	16.17	11.62	13.28
10	2 — " —		Madison	"	1827 – 1849	37	4.71	4.77	4.87
11	1 — " —	(Oxford)	Chenango	"	1829 – 1856	24	4.78	4.72	4.15
12	3 — " —		Otsego	— " —	1826 – 1871	55	9.05	9.69	10.30
	22 Stations in 12 Counties.			Totals:	30	Series.	71.68	64.91	71.44
	" " " " "			Means.			2.39	2.16	2.38

1	3 Stations		Onondaga Co.		1826 – 1858	46	2.22	1.95	2.17
2	2 — " —		Cayuga	"	1827 – 1850	36	2.21	1.82	1.88
3	1 — " —	(Homer)	Cortland	"	1850 – 1863	14	2.80	2.79	2.92
4	1 — " —	Ithaca	Tompkins	"	1828 – 1853	21	2.01	1.60	2.77
5	1 — " —	Sen. Falls	Seneca	— " —	1850 – 1852	3	1.38	2.46	2.91
6	2 — " —		Ontario	— " —	1829 – 1892	35	2.08	2.00	1.87
7	1 — " —	Palmyra	Wayne	— " —	1835	1	1.22	0.85	1.65
8	1 — " —	Mexico	Oswego	— " —	1837 – 1862	24	2.89	2.70	2.80
9	4 — " —		Oneida	— " —	1826 – 1863	52	3.23	2.32	2.66
10	2 — " —		Madison	— " —	1827 – 1849	37	2.36	2.38	2.44
11	1 — " —	Oxford	Chenango	— " —	1829 – 1856	24	2.39	2.36	2.07
12	3 "		Otsego	— " —	1826 – 1871	55	2.26	2.42	2.58
	22 Stations in 12 Counties . . .				Totals:		27.05	25.65	28.72
		Nos. 1 to 12 inclus.			Means for 12 Counties		2.25	2.14	2.39
		Nos. 1 to 11 — " —			" " 11 — " —		2.25	2.11	2.38
		Nos 1 to 10 — " —			" " 10 — " —		2.24	2.09	2.41
		Nos 1 to 8 — " —			" " 8 — " —		2.10	2.02	2.37
		Nos. 1 to 5 — " —			" " 5 "		2.12	2.12	2.53
		Nos. 1 to 4 — " —			" " 4 "		2.31	2.04	2.44
		Nos. 1. to 3 — " —			" " 3 "		2.41	2.19	2.32
		Nos. 1 to 2 — " —			" " 2 "		2.22	1.88	2.02

Apr.	May	June	July	Aug.	Sept.	Oct.	Nov.	Dec.
12.12	13.86	19.10	16.86	15.76	17.34	21.30	14.45	12.22
4.31	7.18	7.32	7.01	6.60	6.31	6.58	4.88	4.84
4.11	4.17	5.47	4.90	3.79	4.00	4.06	3.70	3.23
5.53	6.65	7.16	6.68	6.14	5.74	5.64	4.83	4.79
3.13	2.84	3.15	3.21	1.98	2.69	3.90	3.66	3.46
7.68	9.22	11.26	9.89	9.56	7.77	8.68	7.46	6.25
4.00	0.98	5.61	4.19	4.08	3.27	5.06	1.96	0.93
4.73	5.82	5.81	6.[illegible]	5.84	6.90	7.97	6.85	7.71
16.47	17.02	21.45	23.57	16.21	16.36	18.31	16.96	15.88
4.71	6.69	7.98	7.89	6.28	7.23	6.70	5.54	5.55
6.93	7.35	8.54	8.02	6.14	7.52	6.08	5.95	5.17
13.28	14.06	15.58	15.28	13.79	11.76	14.39	13.08	13.65
87.00	95.34	118.43	113.55	96.17	96.89	108.67	89.32	83.65
2.90	3.18	3.95	3.78	3.21	3.23	3.62	2.98	2.79
2.42	2.67	3.82	3.37	3.15	3.47	4.26	2.89	2.44
2.15	3.59	3.66	3.50	3.30	3.16	3.29	2.44	2.42
4.11	4.17	5.47	4.90	3.79	4.00	4.06	3.70	3.23
2.76	3.33	3.58	3.34	3.07	2.87	2.82	2.42	2.39
3.13	2.84	3.15	3.21	1.98	2.69	3.90	3.66	3.46
2.56	3.07	3.75	3.30	3.19	2.59	2.89	2.49	2.08
4.00	0.98	5.61	4.19	4.08	3.27	5.06	1.96	0.93
2.36	2.91	2.91	3.03	2.92	3.45	3.98	3.43	3.85
3.29	3.40	4.29	4.71	3.24	3.27	3.66	3.39	3.17
2.35	3.34	3.99	3.94	3.14	3.61	3.35	2.77	2.78
3.47	3.67	4.27	4.01	3.07	3.76	3.04	2.97	2.59
3.32	3.51	3.89	3.82	3.45	2.94	3.60	3.27	3.41
35.92	37.44	48.39	45.32	38.38	39.08	43.91	35.39	32.75
2.99	3.12	4.03	3.78	3.20	3.26	3.66	2.95	2.73
2.96	3.09	4.05	3.77	3.17	3.29	3.66	2.92	2.67
2.91	3.03	4.02	3.75	3.19	3.24	3.73	2.91	2.68
2.94	2.94	3.99	3.60	3.18	3.19	3.78	2.87	2.60
2.91	3.32	3.94	3.66	3.06	3.24	3.66	3.02	2.79
2.86	3.44	4.13	3.78	3.33	3.37	3.61	2.86	2.62
2.89	3.48	4.32	3.92	3.41	3.54	3.87	3.01	2.70
2.29	3.13	3.74	3.43	3.28	3.32	3.77	2.66	2.43

Station	County	Period From – To	No. of Years	Jan.	Feb.	Mar.
Means for 5 Stations, in	Onondago + Cayuga Cos. Nos. 1 + 2	1826 – 1858		2.22	1.91	2.09
" " 6 "	Onon., Cay. + Cortland Cos. Nos. 1 + 2 + 3	1826 – 1863		2.29	2.02	2.19
" " 7 "	Onon., Cay., Cort., + Tompkins Co. Nos. 1 + .. + 4	" "		2.23	1.94	2.31
" " 8 " "	Preceding + Seneca Cos. Nos. 1 + ... + 5	" "		2.16	1.99	2.36
" " 12 " "	Prec. + Ontario, Wayne + Oswego Cos. Nos. 1 + .. + 8	1826 – 1892		2.17	2.01	2.28
" " 18 "	Prec. + Oneida + Madison Cos. Nos. 1 + ... + 10	" "		2.41	2.10	2.37
" 19	Prec. + Chenango Cos. Nos 1 + .. + 11	" "		2.41	2.12	2.35
" " 22 " "	Prec. + Otsego Co. Nos. 1 + .. + 12	"		2.39	2.16	2.38
Mean for Stations Nos.	1, 2, 6 + 7 (4 Sta's)	1826 – 1850	17¼	2.20	1.60	1.69
" " "	1, 2, 6, 7, 10 + 11 (6 Sta's)	" – "	17½	2.18	1.70	1.92
" " "	1, 2, 6, 7, 9, 10, 11, 19, 20 + 23 + 25 (11 Sta's)	" – "	16⅔	2.38	2.06	2.12
" " "	1, 2, 6, 7 + 8 (5 Sta's)	1826 – 1850 1850 – 1863	17	2.32	1.84	1.93
Suggested as probable average, from above				2.20	2.10	2.40
"				2.20	2.10	2.40

Apr.	May	June	July	Aug.	Sept.	Oct.	Nov.	Dec.	Monthly Mean. Ins.	Annual Mean. Ins.	
2.35	2.93	3.77	3.41	3.19	3.38	3.98	2.76	2.44		34.57	34.44
2.57	3.09	3.99	3.60	3.27	3.46	3.99	2.88	2.54		35.99	35.87
2.61	3.14	3.90	3.55	3.23	3.34	3.76	2.79	2.51	2.943	35.40 35.[illegible]	[illegible]
2.65	3.11	3.84	3.51	3.12	3.28	3.77	2.87	2.59	2.938	35.34 35.[illegible]	35.25
2.68	2.95	3.82	3.46	3.16	3.18	3.72	2.81	2.55		34.87	
2.78	3.08	3.93	3.76	3.18	3.23	3.67	2.93	2.70		36.17	
2.84	3.13	3.96	3.78	3.17	3.27	3.63	2.93	2.69		36.33	
2.90	3.18	3.95	3.78	3.21	3.23	3.62	2.98	2.79		36.57	
1.97	3.18	3.85	3.63	3.29	3.02	3.19	2.25	2.01		31.88	
2.08	3.28	3.87	3.66	3.23	3.16	3.15	2.48	2.13		32.84	
2.21	3.33	3.80	3.66	3.06	3.18	3.22	2.65	2.40		34.07	
2.40	3.38	4.17	3.89	3.39	3.21	3.36	2.54	2.25		34.68	
2.60	3.20	3.90	3.60	3.30	3.20	3.70	2.80	2.50		35.50	
2.50	3.40	4.00	3.70	3.40	3.30	3.30	2.80	2.40		35.50	

Memoranda relating to Skaneateles Lake.

Mar. 6/96. According to New Atlas of State of New York, published in 1895, the drainage area of the lake above its foot is = 77.125 □ miles.

Max. length of watershed, as per said map, is:	18.625 miles;
-"- width -"- -"- -"- -"- -"-	5.250 -"-;
Mean -"- -"- -"- -"- -"-	4.140 -"-;

Length of lake = 15.0 miles. [Scale of said Map is 2½ miles per Inch.

Mar. 4/96. Stated by Mr. Stone, City Atty, & by Mr. J. N. Tubbs, C.E., that a survey of the watershed of the lake was made by the City Engineer of Syracuse, from which it appears that the total area of the drainage basin is: 73.25 □ miles, of which:

	60.00 □ miles is land surface, and	These figures will be accepted in preference
	13.25 -"- -"- lake -"-.	
Total =	73.25 -"-	

to any other data derived from general maps.

Mr. Stone also states that the rainfall at Homer, Cortland Co., for 20 years, is 45.41" average per year, while that at Auburn, Cayuga Co., for 22 yrs is 34.52" -"- -"-. [The average of these two data is 39.965"; but allowance must be made for prevalence of westerly and northerly winds, from an area of much lower mean annual rainfall. It is also stated that no other rainfall records except those given in the "Regents' Reports" above cited, are available; and it will be noticed that the Homer records are for a later period than the Auburn records. Compare above tables.]

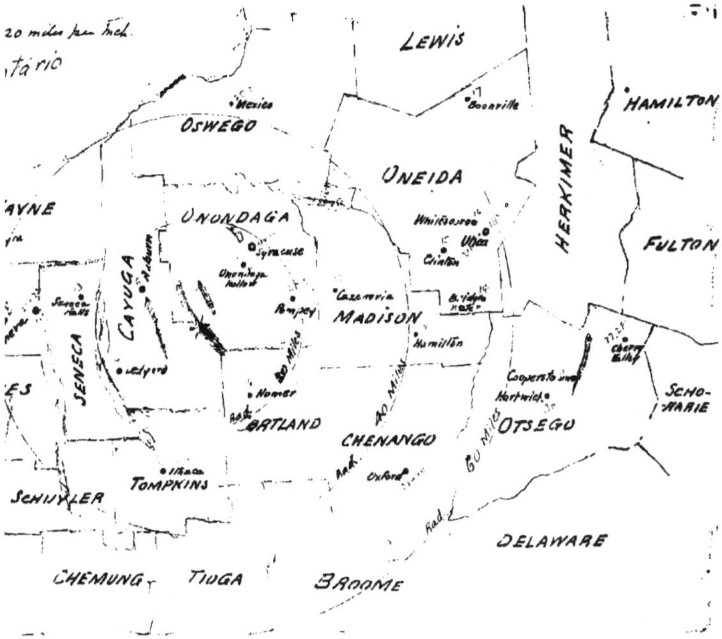
20 miles per Inch
LEWIS
Mexico
Booneville
OSWEGO
HAMILTON
ONEIDA
HERKIMER
AYNE
ONONDAGA
Whitesboro
Utica
Syracuse
Clinton
FULTON
CAYUGA
Auburn
Onondaga Hollow
Seneca Falls
Cazenovia
Bridgewater
Pompey
MADISON
Hamilton
SENECA
Ledyard
80 Miles
Cherry Valley
Cooperstown
Hartwick
SCHO-HARIE
Homer
CORTLAND
40 Miles
OTSEGO
CHENANGO
60 Miles
Oxford
TOMPKINS
Ithaca
SCHUYLER
DELAWARE
CHEMUNG
TIOGA
BROOME

Mar. 7/96. Skaneateles lake lies almost wholly in Onondaga Co., its southern end just reaching Cortland Co., 9 3/8 miles N.N.W. from Village of Homer, while its northern end is 6 7/8 miles E. of Auburn. It also forms practically the dividing line between Cayuga & Onondaga Counties, and is about the center of the area occupied by Onondago, Cortland, Tompkins, Cayuga & the western half of Oswego Counties. The rainfall for these 4 or 5 counties might give an approximation to the rainfall on the watershed of the lake.

French's "Gazetteer" gives elevation of lake at 860 ft. above tide water, and highest summit in township of Spafford, Onondaga Co., at Southern end of lake at 1982 ft. above tide. This is Ripley Hill, 1122 ft. above lake. In the township of Sempronius, Cayuga Co., the highest points are about 1700 ft. above tide. Both of these townships are at Southern part of the lake. To the north, the hills are lower and have easier slopes.

Mar. 9/96 Drive with Mr. Wakefield, Asst Engr., along East side of Watershed from Skaneateles to Homer. — The points referred to by numbers are indicated on blue print map hereto attached; Elevations are from aneroid barometer readings on date, by E.K.

	Top. Elevation above T.W.	Observed altitude	Temp. Degs. F.
Sta. 1. In Main Street of Skaneateles Village at foot of Lake.	860'	1730'	62
" 2. Intersection Main St. & Road to S. on E. Side of Lake	920	1790	60
" 2 + 1/4 mile. Summit in Lake Road on E. " " "	940	1810	58
" 3. Intersection Lake Road & 1st Road to E.	930	1800	54
" 3½ " " " + Shepard's Brook. This is about 30' above lake	890	1765	48
" 4. " " " " + 2nd Road to E.	895	1765	45
" 5 Summit on Road to E. of Sta. 4.	1125	1995	42
" 6 School house on Road " " " ½ mile E. of Sta. 5	1160	2030	42
" 7 Summit on Road to E. of Sta. 4.	1195	2065	41
" 8 Intersection of " " " + Road to S.	1200	2070	41
" 8½. On same Road to S. of Sta. 4, ½ mile E. of Sta. 8	1200	2070	41
" 9. Intersection same Road & main N. & S. Road	1195	2065	40
" 10. On N.&S. Road at Rose Hill P.O. (6 miles from Sta. 1)	1230	2100	37
" 11 " " " Rose Hill "	1275	2145	37
" 12 " " " Intersection E. & W. Road in hollow leading to hills to E.	1150	2020	33
" 12½ " " " ½ mile S. of Sta. 12. (same Hollow as 12)	1090	1960	33
" 13. Borodino Village cross roads	1110	1980	33
" 13a. On Road to S.E. from 13, ½ mile beyond 13	1385	2255	33
" 13b. " " " " 1½ " " "	1490	2360	33

Sta. 13.c. On Road S.E from Sta. 13, + 2 miles from Sta. 13	1540'	2410'	33°F
" 14. " " at E. + W. Road	1585	2455	34
" 14½ " " " " " " (½ mile S.E. of Sta. 14)	1690	2560	34
" 15. " " " " " " Road to W to lake	1740	2610	34
" 16. " " " " " at Spafford. (Cross Roads)	1750	2620	33
" 17. " " S. of Spafford, ⅓ mile S. of Sta. 16. } Hollow	1720	2590	33
" 18. " " " " " ¾ mile " "	1730	2600	33
" 18a " " " " 1 " " "	1720	2590	33
" 18b. " " " " 1½ " " "	1720	2590	32
" 19. " " " " County line + Road to W. opposite head of lake.	1720	2590	32
" 20. " " " " at Road to E. (S. of Co. line)	1720	2590	30
" 21. Junction with N. + S. Road	1660	2530	30
" 22 On N. + S. Road, at Crossing of Scott Brook	1530	2400	30
" 23. Scott Village, Cross Roads. (Stopped to warm) ½ hour	1530	2400	30
{ Barometer kept in sleigh in barn. On starting again about 5⁰⁵ P.M., Barometer began to fall rapidly from 2380' to 2290' at 5¹⁰ P.M., although ground did not fall nearly as fast, being nearly level. For following, we may consider Barometer as = 2290' at Scott.			30
	1530	2290	30
" 23a. On Road S. of Scott village, at Frisbie's house	1505	2265	"
" 23b. " " " " " " " Black's summit	1515	2275	31
" 23c. " " " " " Pickett's " "	1485	2245	31
" 24. " " " " at Creek Crossing (about 2 miles S. of 23) [illegible]	1470	2230	32
" 25. " " " " " Factory Brook Cwg	1420	2180	34
" 26. Junction with road to W. side of lake (forks)	1420	2180	34
" 27 + 28 " " roads to W. near together	1405	2165	34

Sta. 29.	On Road to Homer, 1 mile S. of Sta. 28, Creek Crossing.	1370.	2130	34
" 30.	Junction with N. & S. Road.	1360	2120	"
" 31.	Crossing of Factory Brook, 1/4 mile S. of Sta. 30	1355	2115	"
" 32.	Junction with main N. & S. Road near D.L.&W.RR. Also Creek Crossing nearby.	1320	2080	35
33.	Main St. of Homer, at Academy	1290	2050	35

__Note.__ The elevation of Homer Academy is given at 1090 to 1100 ft. above tide, in various reports; hence above elevations are doubtful. A sudden and large change in Barometer occurred after leaving Scott village. [illegible] — Homer 1100.

[illegible] Mr. Wakefield pointed out locality where he had located the summit in the [illegible] watershed between Scott & Homer. This seems to be correct. There is, however, a basin or depression in the valley extending about ½ mile S. of this summit, which overflows to south, as determined by levels of Mr. Wakefield. The question is whether the infiltration of this basin, prior to overflowing, flows N. or S.; but the presumption is that it goes to the S., as the ground is lower than to the N.

March 1893. Mr. Wm. R. Hill, Chief Engr. states that he caused an accurate survey of the lake & watershed (or crest line thereof) to be made a few years ago, from which it was computed that

Area of Land surface of water-shed	=	60.28 □ miles;
-"- -"- Lake -"-	=	12.75 -"-
Total Area, Land & Water surface	=	73.03 -"-

On this basis, we will have, for the discharge of 1 inch depth over said surfaces, at uniform rate throughout the year:—

1). From 1 square mile:— $Q = \frac{640 . 43560 . 1/12}{365} . 7.4805 = \begin{cases} 47,613 \text{ galls/day} \\ 6,365 \text{ cft/day} \\ 4.42 \text{ cft/min} \\ 0.07367 \text{ cft/sec.} \end{cases}$

or: $Q = (6365 . 7.4805) = \begin{cases} 47,613 \text{ galls/day, or:} \\ 4.42014 \text{ cft/min.} \end{cases}$

Multiplying the factor for 1 □ mile by above areas, we have:—

2). From 60.28 □ miles land surface, 1 inch depth per year $= Q_2 = \begin{cases} 2,870,112 \text{ galls/day} \\ 266,438 \text{ cft/min.} \end{cases}$

3). -"- 12.75 -"- Water -"- -"- -"- $= Q_3 = \begin{cases} 607,066 \text{ galls/day} \\ 56.355 \text{ cft/min.} \end{cases}$

4). -"- 73.03 -"- Combined -"- -"- -"- $= Q_4 = \begin{cases} 3,477,177 \text{ galls/day} \\ 322.793 \text{ cft/min.} \end{cases}$

The above amounts of land & water surface give the following percentages:—

Land area (= 60.28 □ miles)	is	82.54%	of total (73.03 □ miles).
Water -"- (= 12.75 -"-)	-"-	17.46%	-"- -"-
-"- -"- (-"-)	-"-	21.15%	of land (60.28).

With so large a percentage of water surface in lake, on which the evaporation is nearly equal to the rainfall thereon, the total run-off is considerably reduced.

By comparing the monthly evaporation for the 6 months from May to Oct., inclusive, with that for the whole year as found at Boston and elsewhere, we may take said evaporation as being 3/4 of that for entire year; or $\Sigma(e$ for 6 mos. May – Oct.$) = 0.75\,E$, whence $E = \frac{4}{3}\Sigma(e)$ and for Rochester: $E = \frac{4}{3} \cdot 26.79 = 35.72''$, while for Boston we have $E = 3$[illegible]$.05''$. (From above we have for Boston: $E = \frac{4}{3} \cdot 28.76'' = 38.25''$)

For Skaneateles lake, these amounts may be reduced considerably, as evaporation is less in the open lake than in the evap. vessel; lake is also shaded by hills on each side; less sun; colder; circulation of water, — horizontal + vertical; wave action; no reflection of heat from sides of evap. vessel; mists acting as screen to check evaporation; sheltered also from high winds at water surface, &c. May make reduction 10% and take total $= 33.0''$ per year. Note that <u>in winter</u> we may have more evaporation from lake than from vessel, as lake does not freeze over as readily as a small vessel. Perhaps we should take even less than 33.00" owing to coolness of water in Summer, and [illegible] slight evaporation in Winter. We may, however, assume the 33.00" for this case, thus obtaining the following distribution by months:—

Jan.	Feb.	Mar.	Apr.	May	June	July	Aug.	Sept.	Oct.	Nov.	Dec.	Total.
0.6	1.0	1.8	2.5	3.5	4.5	5.0	5.0	4.0	3.0	1.5	0.6	33.00"

Collection of Water per Month.

Let r = monthly rainfall in inches;
e = " evaporation " "
p = " percentage of rainfall collected from land surface.
A_1 = land area in square miles = 60.28 □ miles
A_2 = Water " " " " = 12.75 "
Q_1 = yield of land area in gallons per day
Q_2 = " " water " " "

1 month = 30 days.

$A_2 = 0.2115 A_1$

$$Q_1 = A_1 \cdot \frac{640 \cdot 43560}{30} \cdot \frac{r}{12} \cdot \frac{p}{100} = 774.4 \cdot A_1 rp \text{ in cub. ft. per day}$$

$$Q_2 = A_2 \cdot \frac{640 \cdot 43560}{30} \cdot \frac{r-e}{12} = 77,440 \cdot A_2 (r-e) = 16,378.56 \cdot A_1 (r-e) \text{ cft/day}$$

or: $Q_0 = (Q_1 + Q_2) = 77,440\, A_1 \left(\frac{rp}{100} + 0.2115(r-e)\right)$ cub. ft. per day.

or: $$Q_0 = \begin{cases} 46,680.8\,(rp + 21.15(r-e)) & \text{in cub. ft. per day.} \\ 349,196\,(rp + 21.15(r-e)) & \text{in galls. " "} \end{cases}$$

Note. The elevation of Skaneateles Lake is + 860 ft. above Tide Water.
" " " Owasco " + 670 ft. " "
" " " Otisco " + [illegible] " "

The first-named lake is therefore the highest, and there may be some percolation through the shale rock to both Owasco & Otisco lakes. [illegible] also fact of loss of water in Skaneateles [illegible].

Mean Temperatures & Direction of Wi

From Meteorological Tables published in Reports of "Reg
of State of New York in 1855 & 1872.

{ Note. Small fi
are num
period o

Station.	Mean Temperature F°	No. of days per Month. Red figures are Percen						
		N.	N.E.	E.	S.E.	S.	S.W.	W
1. Auburn 1827–49. (22 yrs)	4[illegible].62	3.19	1.10	0.38	2.26	6.98	5.91	2.
2. Ledyard 18[illegible]–50 (13 yrs)	49.16	5.85	0.67	0.52	1.58	9.49	2.89	3.
3. Onondaga 1826–44 (16 yrs)	47.18	1.56	0.76	1.17	2.15	7.91	2.23	8.
Pompey 1826–43 (17 yrs)	42.83	0.37	0.88	0.19	3.11	4.75	7.69	6.
4. Pompey (1850–70) (5–8 yrs)	44.92	7.6% 534	2.7 190	2.4 165	5.7 400	22.5 1593	16.9 1185	21.
5. Homer. 1832–50 (18 yrs)	44.67	0.07	0.10	0.12	2.30	[illegible].93	8.89	1.
5. Homer. 1850–1860 (12–14 yrs)	4[illegible].3[illegible]	12.1% 1696	1.6 220	2.0 228	16.9 2395	22.6 3167	8.8 1223	18 2
6. Ithaca. 1827–46 (17 yrs)	48.38	[illegible].94	0.95	0.59	2.53	[illegible].85	3.95	8.
6. Ithaca 1850–60 (3–4 yrs)	48.85	11.0 416	4.5 170	6.6 248	18.6 700	20.0 753	11.9 451	9.
Mean of 1–6, inclus.	46.50							
7. Seneca Falls. 1850–70 (3–4 yrs)	45.38	6.6 253	4.7 180	4.1 155	7.1 274	21.9 843	8.1 312	2
8. Geneva 1850–70 (11–14 yrs)	[illegible].09	6.1 725	3.9 472	5.0 597	10.5 1252	24.6 2915	9.9 1180	20
9. Canandaigua 1829–38 (10 yrs)	45.73	1.12	0.50	0.59	1.24	7.91	4.22	10.
10. Mexico 1837–49 (11 yrs)	44.08	2.07	0.89	1.52	4.88	3.[illegible]	2.86	9.
10. Mexico 1850–70 (10–11 yrs)	45.13	8.3 890	2.9 310	5.0 533	27.5 2938	10.2 1094	8.0 872	20
11. Cazenovia 1830–49 (19 yrs)	43.65	0.88	0.51	0.56	1.82	5.27	5.83	5.
12. Utica 1826–48 (23 yrs)	45.68	0.14	0.15	6.30	2.39	1.90	2.35	10
12. Utica 1850–70 (7–8 yrs)	52.18	7.7 531	3.7 258	27.4 1896	7.3 508	4.6 316	4.2 296	3 2
13. Clinton Ham. College. 1850–70 (10–11 yrs)	45.32	5.0 551	1.6 183	11.0 1226	2.2 252	16.7 1874	9.8 1094	4.

From the map of the State, we find that the distances of the principal stations from the middle of the drainage area of Skaneat-eles lake are as follows :— (also Elevations above Tide in Red.)

					Elevation above Tide.
1).	Auburn :	distance =	14.0 miles ;	direction = N. W.	650'
2).	Ledyard	"	18.0 "	" S. W.	447'
3).	Onondaga	"	14.5 "	" N. E.	
4).	Pompey	"	19.0 "	" N. of E.	1300'.
5).	Homer	"	16.0 "	" S. E.	1100'.
6).	Ithaca	"	28.0 "	" W. of S.	417'.
7).	Seneca Falls	"	24.0 "	" N. of W.	400' (?)
8).	Geneva	"	32.0 "	" "	567'.
11).	Cazenovia	"	27.0 "	" N. of E.	1260'
13).	Clinton	"	48.5 "	" "	950'.
12).	Utica	"	57.5 "	" "	424'. Canal
10).	Mexico	"	42.5 "	" E. of N.	330'.
9).	Canandaigua	"	48.0 "	" N. of W.	815'.

From table on preceding page, we have :—

1)	Mean Temperature at Auburn	for 22 yrs	=	46.62 °F.
2.	" " " Ledyard	" 13 "	"	49.16 "
3.	" " " Onondaga	" 16 "	"	47.18 "
4.	" " " Pompey	" 24 "	"	43.44 "
5.	" " " Homer	" 31 "	"	44.13 "
6.	" " " Ithaca	" 20 "	"	48.45 "
	Totals	126		278.98 "
	Mean for 21 yrs.		=	46.50 °F.

For the Wind direction, we also have :—

1).	Resultant direction at Auburn	for 22 yrs	=	S. 73°-14' W.
2).	" " " Ledyard	" 13 "	=	S. 73-01 W.
3)	" " " Onondaga	" 16 "	=	[illegible]-17 W.
4)	" " " Pompey	" 24 "	=	S. 67-[illegible] W.
5)	" " " Homer	" 31 "	=	S. 64-23 W.
6).	" " " Ithaca	" 20 "	=	S. 72-26 W.
	Totals	" 126 "	=	S. 423-01 W.
	Mean for 21 yrs		=	S. 70°-33' W.

Rainfall Records.

It will be sufficient in this case to consider the rainfall stations within a radius of about 20 miles from the middle of the drainage area of the lake. This will bring in the following records:—

1).	At Auburn,	Cayuga Co.	1827–1849	22 yrs.	R =	34.52"	*
	" "	" "	1884–1888	5 "	"	34.11	†
2).	" Sennett.	" "	1827–1850	7 "	"	33.10	*
3).	" Onondaga	Onondaga Co.	1826–1844	16 "	"	31.39	*
4).	" Pompey	" "	1826–18[illegible]	15 "		29.46	*
	" "	" "	1850–1858	9 "	"	3[illegible].94	*
5).	Homer	Cortland Co.	1832–1850	18 "		44.73	*
	" "	" "	1851–1862	12 "	"	45.37	*
	" "	" "	1863–1870	8 "	"	45.85	†
6).	" Ithaca	Tompkins Co.	1828–1848	17 "	"	3[illegible].89	*
	" "	" "	1850–1853	4 "	"	35.14	*
	" "	" "	18[illegible]–18[illegible]2	3[illegible] "	"	34.54	§

* Denotes records given in Regents of Univ. Report.
† " " " " Given in evidence.
§ " " " " N.Y. State Weather Bureau report. 1894.

Of the above, the classification by N.Y. State Weather Bureau is as follows:— Stations 3, 4 & 5 in Eastern Plateau.
" 2 & 6 in Central Lake Region.
" 1 in Great " " .

	Feb.	Mar.	Apr.	May	June	July	Aug.	Sept.	Oct.	Nov.	Dec.	Total.
7	2.20	2.20	2.27	3.36	3.59	3.47	3.34	3.14	3.36	2.99	2.76	35.27
9	1.60	1.26	1.78	3.08	4.21	4.12	3.19	2.93	3.23	2.10	1.57	30.76
1	1.49	1.82	2.12	3.20	3.74	3.12	3.62	2.76	3.10	2.66	1.99	31.63
7	2.76	3.10	3.77	4.09	5.02	4.59	4.00	4.70	3.69	3.82	3.17	45.58
8	2.00	2.23	1.98	3.88	3.81	3.85	3.45	2.76	3.40	2.59	2.41	34.65
1	1.76	2.51	3.00	3.54	3.83	3.31	2.99	3.40	3.25	2.87	2.27	34.54
1	1.97	2.19	2.49	3.52	4.03	3.74	3.43	3.28	3.34	2.84	2.3[illegible]	35.41
0	2.10	2.40	2.50	3.40	4.00	3.70	3.40	3.30	3.30	2.80	2.40	35.50

Run-Offs.

P = Percentages of Rainfall collected.
R = Rainfall in Inches.

	Feb.	Mar.	Apr.	May	June	July	Aug.	Sept.	Oct.	Nov.	Dec.	Total.
- 3	80 4.15	[illegible]1 3.97	101 3.36	53 3.63	29 3.44	17 4.63	26 4.62	25 4.08	26 4.13	41 4.17	57 3.95	[illegible].7 48.38
1 8	78.2 4.06	109.6 4.58	10[illegible].1 3.32	62.3 3.20	29.1 2.98	8.9 3.74	13.0 4.23	14.2 3.23	23.1 4.41	[illegible] 4.11	[illegible] 3.71	[illegible] 45.80
	83	[illegible]3	80	42	25	18	31	28	25	49	[illegible]1	[illegible].2 47.46
	93	112	72	33	17	13	19	19	20	44	74	[illegible] 49.23
	112	13[illegible]	82	37	21	17	24	3[illegible]	2[illegible]	[illegible]7	72	[illegible]7.3 [illegible].13
2 7	11[illegible] 1.70	111.0 1.62	73.5 2.23	49.4 3.43	34.5 3.00	[illegible].7 3.06	12.8 2.85	[illegible].1 2.39	15.7 2.30	28.1 1.92	58.6 1.51	[illegible].94 27.58
0	[illegible] 2.10	[illegible] 2.40	[illegible] 2.50	[illegible] 3.40	[illegible] 4.00	[illegible] 3.70	15 3.40	[illegible] 3.30	25 3.30	[illegible] 2.80	[illegible] 2.40	[illegible] 35.50

Rainfall Records (Continued).

There are several small errors in the foregoing rainfall records, especially in those for Homer. By correcting these errors from the original figures we obtain the following results:–

1). Auburn, for 27 yrs, 1827–1849 & 1884–1889. mean $R = 35.35''$

2). Ledyard – " – 7 " 1827–1850 – " – – " – 33.10

3). Onondaga – " – 16 " 1826–1844 – " – – " – 31.39

4). Pompey 24 – " – 1827–1844 & 1850–1858 – " – – " – 32.85

5). Homer " 38 – " – 1832–1850 & 1850–1870 – " – – " – 45.08

177.77

6). Ithaca. – " – 19 – " – 1830–1874 (St.W.B.) – " – – " – 34.54

212.31

Mean of 1 to 5 inclus. = $35.55''$ ‖ Mean of 1 to 6 inclus. $35.38''$

From this and the foregoing, it is evident that we may take for the Skaneateles Lake district: $R = 3$[illegible]

From the preceding list of Run-off percentages, on preceding page, we also see that it will be fair to adopt $P = 50.0\%$, as the drainage area is better than the Sudbury River area & the Hemlock lake area, but is not quite as good as the Croton river area; also because we have a large percentage of water surface & loss by evaporation therefrom.

Month	Mean Rainfall in Inches. (r)	Mean Collection in Per Cent. (p)	Mean Evaporation from Lake in Inches. (e)	Factor [rp + 21.15(r−e)]	Ratio of mean Collection to monthly Collection.	$\left(\frac{rp}{100}\right)$ Inches	r−e Ins.
Jan.	2.2"	60.	0.6"	165.84		1.32"	+1.60"
Feb.	2.1	100.	1.0	233.77		2.10	+1.10
Mar.	2.4	120.	1.8	300.69		2.88	+0.60
April	2.5	100.	2.5	250.00		2.50	0.00
May	3.4	60.	3.5	201.89		2.04	−0.10
June	4.0	40.	4.5	[illegible]		1.60	−0.50
July	3.7	20.	5.0	46.50		0.74	−1.30
Aug.	3.4	15.	5.0	17.16		0.51	−1.60
Sept.	3.3	20.	4.0	51.30		0.66	−0.70
Oct.	3.3	25.	3.0	[illegible]		0.83	+0.30
Nov.	2.8	40.	1.5	139.50		1.12	+1.30
Dec.	2.4	60.	0.6	182.07		1.44	+1.80
Totals.	35.5	50.	33.0	1827.88 $\frac{1}{12}$ = 152.32	1.00	17.74	[illegible]

For the yield of the entire water-shed, (land + water surfaces) we have:

$$Q_0 = 349,196\,[rp + 21.15(r-e)] \text{ galls per day} = [illegible]$$

$$46,680.8\,[rp + 21.15(r-e)] \text{ cub. ft. per day} =$$

$$32,417\,[rp + 21.15(r-e)] \text{ cub. ft. per min.} = 4937.78 \text{ cft/min}$$

$$0.540278\,[rp + 21.15(r-e)] \text{ cub. ft. per sec.} = 82.2965 \text{ cft/sec.}$$

Desmond FitzGerald, C.E., of Boston, was also put on the witness stand, and testified as follows:— Area of watershed is 60.25 □ miles of land surface + 12.75 □ miles lake surface = 73.00 □ miles. Rainfall, from Report of State Weather Bureau, 1894, is from 30" to 36" per year, on average; use for this mean depth = 33"; of which 47%, or 15.5" may be collected in lake, thus giving mean yield of 5[illegible],1[illegible]3,000 gallons per day. This includes the yield from both land and water surface of entire area. The water surface alone will yield a little over 5,000,000 galls/day. As this estimate may be [illegible] somewhat, we may say that the area will yield from 50 to 60 million galls/day. The data collected by Cons. Engr. Wm. R. Hill, of Syracuse indicate that the rainfall at Skaneateles Village (foot of lake) is 31.69" and that the run-off is 46%, but this is only for a very few years, and hence we may find both larger and smaller values. Evaporation from the water surface of lake may here be regarded as balanced by the rainfall, so that in computing the yield, the water surface may be omitted from calculation.

Cross-examination. In the [illegible] since established, the rainfall is measured at 5 different places now, and formerly at only 2 places. Am not satisfied with only 1 gauge, and in Skaneateles watershed it should demand several gauges, to be set on broad [illegible] area, give them [illegible] elevation. One gauge is vastly better

J. C. Vermeule's formula for loss by evaporation in general, as given in his report on "Water Supply" in Report of Geolog. Survey of New Jersey. 18[illegible].

E = annual amount of water lost by evap., percol. &c. in inches (mean).
R = " " " rainfall in inches. (mean).
T = mean temperature of locality in degrees F.; then:

$$E = (15.50 + 0.16R)(0.05T - 1.48).$$

Based on data from the watersheds of the Passaic, Croton & Sudbury rivers.

Let us now see what the value of T must be to make $E = R$, whereby there would be no water running off at all.

For convenience place: $15.50 = a$; $0.16 = b$; $0.05 = c$; and $1.48 = d$; then formula becomes: $E = (a + bR)(cT - d)$, and placing $E = R$, we get:

$$R = acT - ad + bcTR - bdR, \text{ or:}$$

$$T(ac + bcR) = R(1 + bd) + ad, \text{ or: } t = T = \frac{R(1+bd) + ad}{ac + bcR} =$$

or $$T = \frac{1.2368R + 22.940}{0.008R + 0.775}.$$

For $R = 36''$, we thus find: $T = \frac{64.465}{1.063} = 63.5^{\circ}$ F. to give $E = R$.

Applying the above formula to the [illegible] district, and taking mean values of T & R at Stations No. 1, 2, 3, & [illegible], we arrive at:

$T = 46.47^{\circ}$ say 46.5° F.; $R = 35.55''$, we obtain:

$E = (15.50 + 0.16R)(0.05T - 1.48) = 17.897''$ say $17.90''$, thus leaving the Run-off: $R - E = (35.55 - 17.9) = 17.65''$ or 49.6% of R.

B. R. & P. R.R. Co. Case at Colden, N.Y.

May 7. 1896

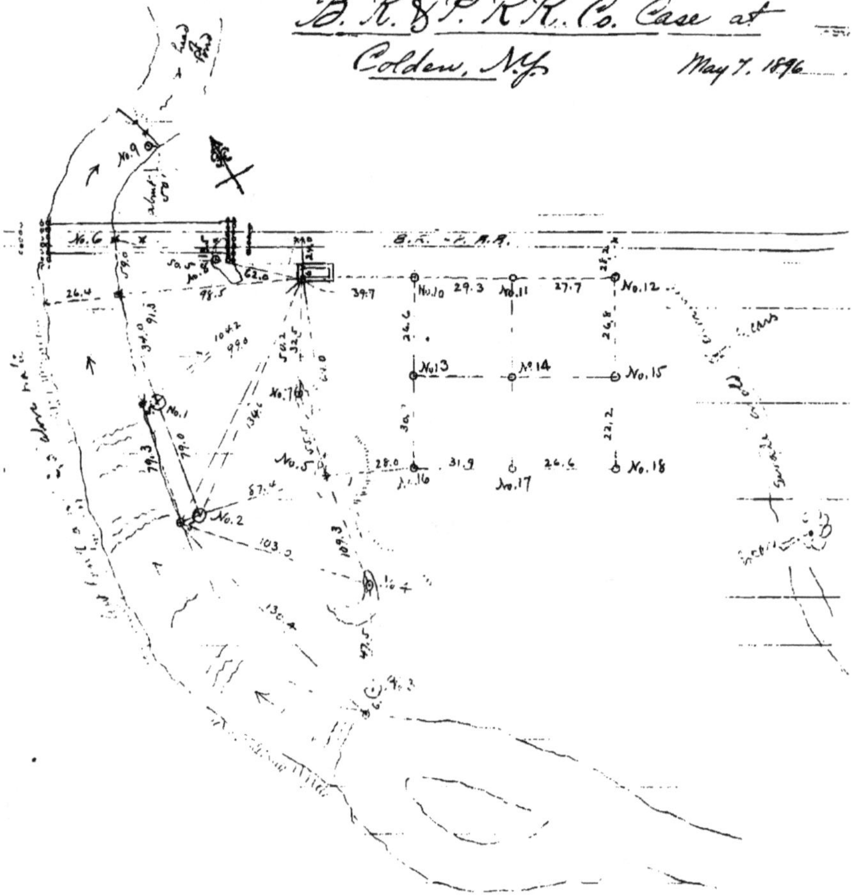

B.M.	On Timber of E. Abutment of R.R. Bridge.	1.[illegible] P.M.	4.690		
6	Peg at E. edge of Creek	[illegible] "	8.025 Water	Fall in Water Surface at 3.31 P.M. was 1/2"	8.067
8	Peg in pool at E. abutment	[illegible] "	7.880 Water	" " " 3.22 " " 1"	7.960
7	" " " S.W. of Well	1.07 "	7.620 Water	" " " 3.22 " " 2½"	7.830
1	" " Pit at creek	12.55 "	7.875 Water	" " " " " 3.30 " " [illegible]"	7.896
1	" " E. edge of Crk	"	7.780 Water	" " " " 3.30 " " [illegible]"	8.011
2	" " Pit at creek	12.52 "	7.620 Water	" " " " 3.27 " " [illegible]"	7.651
2	" " E. edge of Crk	"	7.770 Water	" " " " 3.27 " " [illegible]"	7.8[illegible]1
3	Stone in Pit at creek	12.[illegible] "	[illegible] Water	6.580 Water [illegible] | about same at 3.25 P.M.	6.580
3	Peg in E. edge of crk	"	5.920 Water	5.935 Water at 12.58 P.M. | 5.960 [illegible] at [illegible] P.M. || 5.980 at 3.25 P.M.	5.9[illegible]
4	" " pool.	12.50 "	[illegible] Water	Fall in water surface at 3.24 P.M was [illegible]"	6.800
5	" "	1.[illegible] "	7.280 Water	" " " " 3.23 " " 2⅜"	7.480
19	Top of [illegible] in Curb N.W. Cor. Well.	1.12 "	4.[illegible]		
20	Water surf. in Well.	"	7.270 Water	10.960 Water at 3.4[illegible] P.M. (Reduced 3.69 ft.) [illegible]	10.960
10	[illegible] of 2" [illegible]	1.15 "	5.[illegible] + 2.303 = 7.[illegible]	From top pipe to water at 3.37 P.M. = 2.40'	7.[illegible]
11	" " "	1.17 "	5.[illegible] + 2.090 = 7.[illegible]	" " " " 3.42 P.M. = 2.[illegible]	7.[illegible]
12	" " "	1.18 "	3.[illegible] + [illegible] = 7.140	" " " " 3.[illegible] = [illegible]	7.32[illegible]
13	" " "	1.23 "	3.[illegible] + 3.[illegible] = 7.[illegible]	" " " " 3.[illegible] p.m = 3.69	7.650
14	" " "	1.22 "	[illegible] + [illegible] = 7.2[illegible]	" " " 3.[illegible] " 3.35	7.36[illegible]
15	" " "	1.19 "	[illegible] + 2.[illegible] = 7.3[illegible]	" " " 3.47 " [illegible].89	[illegible]
16	" " "	1.24 "	2.[illegible] + [illegible] = 7.22[illegible]	" " " " 3.52 p.m = [illegible]	7.[illegible]
17	" " "	1.[illegible] "	[illegible] + 3.[illegible] = 7.210	" " " " 3.[illegible] " 3.26	7.[illegible]
18	" " "	1.2[illegible] "	3.[illegible] + 3.23[illegible] = 7.[illegible]	" " " " 3.[illegible] " 3.33	7.2[illegible]

May 7, 18[illegible]. **Notes on B. R. & P. RR. Case.**

A peg was also driven in creek near small weir N. of RR. bridge about 1.40 P.M., nail even with water surface, & soon after we went to dinner. The elevations of peg & weir, &c. were taken on our return, and are as follows: Peg = 8.100 below ⊼ as on preceding page, properly reduced to B.M. (This is also water surface at 1.40 P.M.); Weir crest (board) = 8.330 mean; Water surface at 3.32 P.M. = 8.070; same at 4.30 P.M. = 8.025

Length of weir, = 9.70'; 2 end contractions, but little or no bottom contraction. Water volume in creek reduced about 1½ P.M. somewhat, due to shutting down of mills above. Depth on weir may be taken at 0.30', as max., hence: $Q = 3.33 \cdot l h^{3/2} = \frac{10}{3} \cdot 9.7 \cdot .3 \cdot 0.55 = 5.33$ cft/sec., or from 5 to 6 cft/sec.

At 3½ P.M., a gauging of flow in mill race (flume) was made, by velocity observations; width of channel = 7.50'; depth from 9½" to 11½"; mean of depths = 10.6" = 0.883 ft; mean area of water section = 6.6225 □ft; max. velocity = 1.00 ft/sec.; hence mean velocity = 0.85% of max. velocity; or $Q = Av = 6.62 \cdot 0.85 = 5.63$ cft/sec. There was at this time but little leakage through or over mill dam, the latter being only about 4½ ft. high. The leakage did not exceed by estimate 0.5 cft/sec. in all; hence flow of creek at said hour was about 6.0 cft/sec., which agrees fairly with estimate from weir measurement at about 4.30 pm., since latter may be increased about 10% owing to absence of bottom contraction and to leakage through sod & weir. Possibly the leakage through & over mill-dam may have been somewhat more than above estimated, viz: 0.5 c#/sec., at the hour when the gauging was made, but it was certain; not over 1.0 c#/sec. then. When we first arrived at said dam, there was much more flow over crest, but probably the mill-wheel was then shut down temporarily and was opened while we were absent going down the stream. We may therefore say that the discharge of the stream did not exceed <u>6.50 c#/sec.</u> on date.

<u>Operation on grounds.</u> — Arrived from Buttle's about 11^{00} AM., May 7 '96. At 11^{20} AM. took sample of water from well; (sample marked No 1. Water perfectly clear + cool, temperature after 15^{m} immersion in well being 52°F. Temperature of water in Creek at 11^{35} AM. was 69°F., that of the air being somewhat lower. Day bright + pleasant, strong sunshine, and stream being quite shallow. After arrival, pits nos. 1, 2 + 3 were dug on East side of creek, near edge of water; the soil was sand + gravel, and water entered freely from sides to fill said pits, although the principal flow appeared to come from the land (E.) side in all cases. Muddy water was bailed out from said pits and after filling with clear water by infiltration, about 1/4 lb <u>Eosine</u> (Aniline Red) was put in each pit, in the water, which was thereby dyed a bright red. The chemical was in its original sealed package + was opened by Mr. Wm. E. Hoyt, Chf Engr, in my presence. The dye was applied by me as follows: In pit No. 1 at 12^{00} M.; in pit No 2, at 12^{15} P.M.; in pit No. 3 at 12^{30} P.M. In pits No. 1 + 2, the water was thus

at, or slightly [illegible], creek level, while in pit No. 3 it appeared to be stationary at about 6" below creek level. (This pit No. 3 did not fill higher at any time later).

The dye made its appearance unmistakeably in the creek at Pit No. 1, at 12^{20} P.M., and at Pit No. 2 at 12^{35} P.M., but did not show at any point from Pit No 3, during entire afternoon. The quantity of dye was so large that it sufficed to furnish color for entire period from Nos. 1 & 2. In No. 3, the water seemed to become clearer in course of afternoon, although there was no visible inflow or outflow from pit, nor did it appear to rise or fall perceptibly; but the marked difference in appearance between water in No. 3, and that in Nos. 1 & 2, led me to infer a subterranean communication without visible outlet. In both 1 & 2, the water retained its greenish fluorescence in certain lights, while in No 3, it became much clearer during afternoon.

Up to 1^{40} P.M., the water in the well was frequently examined, but no trace of color was detected therein. No pumping from well had been done since the previous day and no visible outflow from well was found, water level therein being stationary. At 1^{35} P.M., the pump was started at full speed so as to lower water level in well as rapidly as possible and to induce the greatest attainable filter head on the subsoil water.

The pump was a piston pump [illegible]" cylinder x [illegible]" stroke and making 60 strokes per min., which rate was reduced somewhat later in afternoon as water fell to avoid losing suction.

__Water Tank.__ The water tank, about 400' E. of Pump, (latter being located near E. abutment of bridge & on N. side of R.R. bank) is a wooden cistern 24' diam. at base × 16' high, and has a rated capacity of 50,000 gallons. Assume dimensions and taper as in adjoining sketch, giving [illegible] = 49,000 galls. approx.

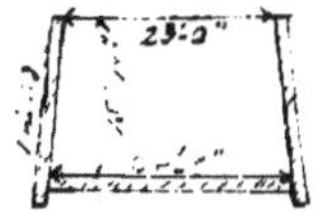

At 1^{30} P.M., water was 4.95' deep in tank; Pumping began at 1^{35} P.M.; at 3^{15} P.M., depth was 7.70', and an Engine had taken in meantime a depth of $\left\{ \begin{matrix} 1\frac{5}{8}" \\ 0.14' \end{matrix} \right\}$; at 4^{45} P.M. depth was 10.25' and another Engine had meanwhile taken about 1500 galls. of water = 200 cu.ft. = depth of 0.46'; Total rise of water = $(\underbrace{10.25 + 0.46 + 0.14}_{10.85} - 4.95) =$ [illegible]'. Diam. at depth = 4.95' is $23\frac{2}{3}$' say 23.7'; diam. at depth = 10.85' is [illegible].28, say [illegible]; mean diam. = 23.[illegible]'; area = 434. sq.ft.; volume = 434 × [illegible] = 2560 cu.ft. = [illegible] galls. Time of pumping = $(4^{45} - 1^{35}) = 3^h 10^m =$ [illegible] min.; mean rate = [illegible] galls. per min., = [illegible] cu.ft./min.

Dimensions of well, inside vertical timber sides, are 13.24' × 6.[illegible]'; rectangular; area = [illegible].44 sq.ft.; [illegible] = [illegible] (2.7 − 4.[illegible]) = 3.17' below timber curb at N.W. cor.; at 4^{45} P.M. it was 6.77' below same point; fall in $3^h 10^m$ = 190 min. was then (6.77 − 3.17) = 3.60', and [illegible] volume [illegible] by pumping, exclusive of inflow, was: [illegible] × 3.60 = 2[illegible].4 cu.ft.

Inflow to well was as follows: from [illegible] to [illegible] P.M., = [illegible] min., rise was about (6.77 − 6.30) = 0.47', or at rate of about 0.08' = 1" per min., after pumping was stopped; and from 5^{00} to 5^{10} P.M., (by watch) in exactly 10 min., the rise was 5 11/16" = 0.474 ft, or at rate of 0.0474' per min; and during 1st 5 min., from 5^{00} to 5^{05}, the rise was 2 63/64" = 2.984" = 0.2487 ft, or at rate of 0.04974 ft per min. The rate of inflow thus diminishes rapidly as the well fills, and is greatest at bottom. **Assume rate at bottom = 0.05 ft per min., or at rate of: $q = at$ = 79.44 × 0.05 = 3.972 cft/min., or say 4.00 cft/min., with average rate of 2.00 cft/min. while well is being rapidly pumped out. The lowest stage of the water was noticed at 3^{40} p.m., when it stood 6.88' below curb, its initial stage at 1^{35} P.M. being 3.19' below curb. We thus have a fall of (6.88 − 3.19) = 3.69' in the period of 125 min from 1^{35} to 3^{40} P.M., with an inflow of 250 cft during said time, thus making total volume pumped = {(79.44 × 3.69) + 250} = (293.1 + 250) = 543.1 cft. Add to this the inflow at rate of 4.0 cft/min., during period from 3^{40} to 4^{45} P.M. = 65 min, being 260 cft, we have total of (543 + 260) = 803 cft, as against about 2560 cft as per tank measurement above. This shows that there is either some error in the tank measurement or the data relating to the well.**

As to the tank, we may assume that one of the locomotives took less than [illegible] gals = 200 cft, and that total volume put therein was not over about 2500 cft. Deduct from this the volume in the well, viz: 293 cft, thus leaving 2207 cft to be furnished by infiltration to well & pumping therefrom during the period from 1^{35} to 4^{45} P.M = 190^{min}, which is at rate of $\frac{2207}{190} = 11.616$ cft/min.

This is, however, much larger than the rate of inflow from [illegible] P.M. as per close measurement above, viz: $(79.44 \times 0.0474) = 3.765$ cft/min., or even than the preceding approximate measurement from $4^{[illegible]}$ to 5^{3} giving 0.47' rise in 6^{min}, or a rate of $\frac{79.44 \times 0.47}{6} = 6.223$ cft/min.

It therefore follows that the independent gravity supply to said tank must have been in strong operation at the time, and hence all data relating to tank must be rejected.

Tank records are as follows:— { Pumping began at 1^{35} P.M. / " " stopped at 4^{45} P.M }

Water level stood at depth of 4.95' at 1^{30} P.M. } During this interval an,
" " " " 7.75' " $3^{[illegible]}$ " } [illegible] 1903 – 2.14'
" " " " 10.25' " $4^{[illegible]}$ " } Engine took about 1600 [illegible]

Well records are as follows:— (Pumping as above.)

Water level stood at 3.19' below curb at $1^{[illegible]}$ P.M. } low level [illegible]
" " " " [illegible] " " " $[illegible]^{40}$ " } [illegible]
" " " " 6.77' " " " 4^{47} " } [illegible]
" " " " [illegible] " " " [illegible] " } [illegible]

The coloration of water in well was first noticed at $4^{[illegible]}$ p.m., [illegible] frequent dippings were taken. At this hour, $4^{[illegible]}$ p.m., some Eosine was put into pipe No. [illegible], and about $4^{[illegible]}$ a hole was made in ground adjacent to said [illegible], on the south side thereof. The ground water, which was about 10' below surface, & this was also dyed with Eosine. First faint coloration of water in well was noticed at 5^{00} p.m. The complete record of observations on Well, we may state that when water was first seen at its lowest level, time 3 P.M., a good inflow thro' a bolt hole in the timber, at or near the N.E. Cor. was observed, and a smaller inflow at 2 places on the W. side, all about 6.3' to 6.5' below curb. This inflow continued during entire time that water was maintained at low level. Bottom of well was not observed, as it contained nearly 1' depth of water at lowest stage.

There is little reason to believe that this color in the well came from the Eosine in Pits Nos. 1 2 + 3, but excellent reason for believing that it came from the dye put in Well or Pipe No. 10, about 26' E., thus showing a current in the ground water from land to creek instead of the reverse. It would have been better to have used a different color in Pipe No. 11 from that used in Pits Nos. 1, 2 + 3.

Pipes or Wells Nos. 13 – 18. A group of 7 2" pipes, about 8' long, was driven into the ground, as indicated on map, to the East & South of the large pumping well. Instead of being open on bottom, the lower ends of these pipes were hammered together to form an edge, and numerous chisel slots were cut in sides above edge to admit water, the workmen considering that a sort of strainer would thus be formed at each pipe. Most of the pipes were thus entered before our arrival on ground.

The communication between ground water outside and that inside of said pipes was not free in the case of Pipe No. 10, as was proven by the failure of an additional quantity of water put therein at about 4[00] P.M. to escape by even 5[10] P.M. This remained standing in said pipe fully 1½ ft above ground water level. There was probably a similar action in the other wells or pipes, so that no good indication of the fall in the ground water level was secured by the lowering of the water level in the main well. After pumping on [illegible] the fall [illegible] was found:— In No. 10 / 0.15'; No. 11 / 0.03'; No. 12 / 0.15'; No. 13 / 0.04'; No. 14 / 0.07'; No. 15 / 0.02'; No. 16 / 0.34'; No. 17 / 0.12'; No. 18 / 0.13'.

Open Pools of Stagnant water, in flood Channel. Pegs were driven in 4 open pools in flood channel of Creek, flush with water surface before beginning to pump. There was no communication between said pools visible on surface. Pools or pegs were numbered No. 4, 5, 7 & 8, located as per map. Bottom of flood channel was sand & gravel. Pegs were from 2' to 3' long. Initial water level indicated by nail head. Fall in water level after pumping was found by measuring down from said nail head to water surface. Pumping began at 1[35] P.M., and at from 3[22] to 3[24] P.M., the following falls were observed in said pools:— the 1st 48[min]:—

1" fall at No. 8; 2½" fall at No. 7; 2¾" fall in No. 5, and ½" fall in No. 4. No appreciable fall occurred in pools Nos. 1, 2 & 3, except due to changes of volume in Creek.

Test Pits in Swale S.E. of Well. — There is also a small swale or old arm of creek to the S.E. of Pumping Well, as indicated on map, and in this two excavations were made. The soil in bottom was a thick black silt or mud, cutting like soft clay, for a depth of about 1.5 ft at 1st excavation nearest RR., and about 3.7 ft at second pit, the bottom in both cases being gravelly. The bottom of swale was covered with fine grass, the adjacent land being a flat meadow, with hard clayey soil.

Conclusions. The above test was in general unsatisfactory, owing to failure of the 2" pipes to give correct indication of level of subsoil water, also from shortness of time for the test. Taking the results as recorded above, it is probable that some water is taken from the plainly marked flood channel by percolation into the sump well, but that the larger share of said water comes from the land side, while no water comes directly from the running open stream. The question is therefore how near to the channel of a stream may a well be located without liability for diversion of water, also whether the flood channel is properly a part of the stream in a legal sense. It is not proven by any of our observations that some of the subsoil water does not percolate from the open stream through the underlying gravel and sand to the sump well.

Mill. The mill below the R.R. bridge is equipped with a turbine having a total fall of 25.0' from stream to stream. Probably at least 1.0 head was lost at date through the 2 racks, the long flume & the tail race. The two racks may each give loss of about 0.30'; the tail race has fall of at least 0.60 ft and the flume is about 200 ft. long, and curved, passing obliquely under the street. The fall of 25.0 was determined by Mr. Jordan with level, and it is probably a liberal estimate to take effective head on wheel at 24.0 ft

Pumpage. The present pumping has been done for about 4 yrs. past, the intention being to maintain about 16 ft. depth of water in the tanks; and as the latter is not allowed to become entirely empty, it is fair to conclude that not over 8 ft. depth, or half of the total capacity, is used per day. This would be about 20,000 gallons per day, pumped during the usual working day of 10 hours. The pump is said to be 6" diam. x 10" stroke, making at [illegible] at 60 strokes per minute. Cylinder Capacity is thus:-

$D = 5''$; $\frac{\pi d^2}{4} = A = 19.635\ \square in$; Volume at 10" stroke $= \frac{196.35\ cu\,in}{231\ cu\,in/gall} = 0.85\ gall =$
$= 0.1136\ cft$; and allowing 5% for slip, this would give:-

$V = 0.8075\ galls = 0.1079\ cft$. With 60 strokes per minute the delivery would thus be: $Q = 48.45\ galls/min = 6.474\ cft/min$.

To pump 25000 galls. in 10 hours, requires a rate of:

$$Q = \frac{25000}{10 \cdot 60} = 41.63\ galls/min = 5.57\ cft/min = 0.09283\ cft/sec.$$

This rate of pumping applies directly to the creek and the well, with effective head of 24.0 ft, gives a power of:

$$P = \frac{Qh}{12} = \frac{0.09283 \cdot 24}{12} = 0.1856\ HP$$ for 10 hrs. per day

and as no water is pumped at night, no loss can occur for the other 14 hrs. per day.

From the foregoing, however, the max. rate of inflow to the well, from exact timing & measurement of rise in 10 min, was $Q = 3.765\ cft/min = 0.06275\ cft/sec$. More than this could not be drawn, as rate of infiltration decreases rapidly as water rises in the well, and at max. [illegible] level the pump loses suction. Taking this as the measure of max. abstraction from the stream, without allowance for the water coming from the land side into well, we have the power:- as before:-

Another set of observations was made on May 9. 1896, by Mr. Wm. F. Jordan, Asst Engr., or 2 days after above, and a few additional facts elicited.

Steam pump was started at 10^{30} A.M. May. 9. tank reading 10.00 ft

" " " stopped " 2^{00} P.M. " " " 15.80 ft

The depth of water in tank was thus increased 5.80 ft in 3½ hrs = 210 min; during which time the water in the well was lowered 3.83 ft. Taking diam. of tank (at mean depth of 12.9 ft) at 23.75', the volume pumped in was: $V = 443 \times 5.8 = 2569.4$ cft, no draft therefrom occurring during said time; on the other hand, the volume apparently taken from well was: $13.2' \times 6' = 79.2$ □ft area; say area = 79.0 □ft and depth = 3.83 ft, whence $V = 79 \times 3.83 = 302.6$ cft: The inflow to said well during said time of 210 min must therefore have been $(2569.4 - 302.6) = 2266.8$ cft, or at rate of $q_1 = \frac{2266.8}{210} = 10.794$ cft/min.

<u>Note.</u> { Mr. Jordan is positive that both on this and the previous occasion, there was no contribution from the gravity supply, and that the valve on latter at tank was tightly closed. }

The rate of pumping was: $q_0 = \frac{2569.4}{210} = 12.235$ cft/min. = 91.53 [illegible]

Pump capacity 5" diam. × 10" stroke = [illegible].4 cu. in. = 0.85 galls, and for 1 revolution, or complete out & in stroke, capacity = 1.70 galls. To give 91.53 galls/min, the rate of operation must have been $\frac{91.53}{1.7}$ = = 54 full strokes or revolutions per min. Pump can work 60 or more revols. per min.

From the above & previous pumping record, it follows that a large volume of ground water must be stored around well in order to give discharge computed, also that the effect of this pumpage is slight upon the level of the ground water at some distance beyond well.

Mr. Jordan also observed fall of water in the several pipes and pools previously described, the pipes, however, being pulled out as it was found that the tight [illegible] [illegible] [illegible] [illegible] [illegible] [illegible].

Compare the adjacent diagram with that on p. —— ante.

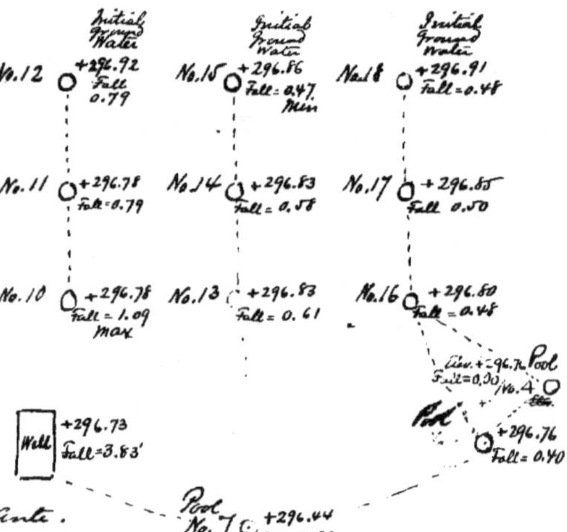

The initial ground water levels were taken just before 10.30 A.M., when pump was started, and the falls in said levels were taken about 4.45 P.M. after water in well had been lowered 3.8[illegible] ft by pumping. The water in Well was maintained at min. level by pumps up to 4.45 P.M.

No elevations were taken of Nos 1, 2 3 & 6. Creek remained uniform throughout the day, and same in stage as on May 7. The pit at No. 3 had not yet filled and water was still 6" below level of creek.

The engineer in charge of the steam pump states that the average daily use of water at this Station has been as follows:–

In 1892,	pumped in aggregate	12 days,	averaging 5.0′ depth in tank
" 1893,	" "	25 "	" 6.0′ " "
" 1894,	" "	60 "	" 6.0′ " "
" 1895,	" "	83 "	" 7.0′ " "
Total in 4 years,		180 "	" 6.4′ " "

Taking diam. of tank on average = 23.8 ft, and area = 444.88 □ft, say = 445 □ft, we have average daily volume pumped = $Q = 2848.0$ cft/day

Assume this volume taken at uniform rate in (n) hours; then

for $n = 10$ hrs, rate of draught is $\frac{2848}{10 \cdot 60} = 4.747$ cft/min $= 0.079$ cft/sec.

" $n = 8$ " " " $\frac{2848}{8 \cdot 60} = 5.934$ " $= 0.099$ "

" $n = 6$ " " " $\frac{2848}{6 \cdot 60} = 7.912$ " $= 0.132$ "

Taking ($n = 8$) as the avg., or a rate of 0.10 cft/sec., for the pumping during said aggregate of 180 days; also allowing effective head of $h = 24$ ft at mill, we have loss of power to mill:–

$$N = \frac{Qh}{12} = \frac{0.10 \cdot 24}{12} = 0.2 \text{ HP} = 1/5 \text{ HP for 180 days.}$$

This amount is very small, being less than the friction on a small amount of machinery in mill. Inattention to bearings of machinery, or poor oiling, will entail a larger loss by friction.

) 90. 45.	5.31 (3) 1.77	130. 43.3
94.	1.99 1.58 3.5- 1.79 (2)	74. 80. 154. 77.
91. 158. 249. 124.5	1.90	82.
97.	—	—
) 44[illegible].) 259. 110. 129.5	5.47 (3) 15.69 (2) 1.82 7.85	236. 119. 78.7 59.5
191. 165 356. 178.	—	—
177.	1.61	166.

4.35	103.	—	—
4.15	105.		
4.24	119.		
4.43	99.		
4.19	94.		
21.36 (5)	520.		
4.27	104.		
34.34 (8)	766.	13.87 (3)	253.
4.29	95.8	4.62	84.3
4.41	49.	—	—
4.08	108.		
4.37	82.		
4.22	58.		
17.08 (4)	297.		
4.27	74.2		
4.28	70.	4.93	105.
4.05	66.	4.61	97.
8.33 (2)	136.	9.54 (2)	202.
4.17	68.	4.77	101.
4.34	155.	4.83	74.
		4.73	80.
		4.58	124.
		14.14 (3)	278.
		4.71	92.7
29.75 (7)	588.	23.68 (5)	480
4.25	84.	4.74	96.
4.43	86.	4.99	81.
4.13	86.	4.91	88.
4.13	118.	4.76	90.
		4.79	105.
		9.55 (2)	195.
		4.78	97.5
12.69 (3)	290	19.45 (4)	364
4.23	96.7	4.86	91.

1.48	50.	1.87	67.6	2.38	73.8	2.75	89.6	3.24
—	—	1.85 1.99 3.84 (2) 1.92	39. 33. 72. 36.0	2.49	33.	—	—	3.16 3.46 6.62 3.31 (2)
—	—	—	—	2.44 2.15 4.59 (2) 2.29	23. 33. 56. 28.0	2.87 2.92 2.54 2.85 11.18 (4) 2.80	18. 11. 27. 13. 69. 17.3	—
—	—	—	—	2.16	23.	2.59 2.83 2.99 8.41 (3) 2.80	36. 10. 22. 68. 22.7	3.03 3.18 6.21 3.11
—	—	3.84 (2)	72.	9.24 (4)	112.	19.57 (7)	137.	12.83 (4
19.32 (3)	138.	7.14 (1)	48	7.62 (1)	36.	17.62 (2)	97.	11.64 (1
—	—	1.92	36.	2.31	28.	2.80	19.6	3.21
		7.14	48.	7.62	36.	8.81	48.5	11.64
1.48	19.	1.62	24.	2.40	39.	—	—	3.02 3.18 3.17 9.37 (3) 3.12
—	—	1.68	5.	2.34	9.	2.55	41.	3.46 3.38 3.20 10.04 (3) 3.35
—	—	1.69	9.	—	—	2.63	20.	3.38 3.20 6.58
1.48 (1) 21.37 (3) 1.48	19. 93. 19.	4.99 (3)	38.	4.74 (2)	48.	5.18 (2)	61.	25.99 (8
		1.66	12.7	2.37	24.	2.59	30.5	3.25

4.55	35.	5.33 5.36 10.69 (2) 5.34	36. 61. 97. 48.5	—	—	6.43 6.59 8.72 11.64
4.89	30.	5.20	29.	5.79 5.83 11.62 (2) 5.81	36. 22. 58. 29.0	7.62 13.49
4.99	76.	5.41	31.	5.55	37.	6.39 7.14 13.53 [illegible].90
14.43 (3)	141	21.30 (4)	157.	17.17 (3)	95.	
4.81	47.	5.33	39.2	5.72	31.7	6.44
4.54	15.	5.26	36.	5.87	13.	7.16

—	—	—	—	2.30 2.10 2.28 6.68	10. 5. 8. 23.	—	—
—	—	1.60 (1)	8.	13.05(6)	48.	5.70 (2)	29.
15.52 (2)	31.	32.81(4)	107.	8.63 (1)	24.	18.41(2)	54.
—	—	1.60	8.	2.18	8.	2.85	14.5
7.76	15.5	8.20	26.8	8.63	24.	9.20	27.0
1.44 1.21 2.65	24. 28. 52.	—	—	2.24	15.	2.76 2.70 2.73 8.19	52. 28. 21. 101
—	—	1.60	9.	—	—	2.68	12.
1.09	9.	1.63	11.	2.04	6.	—	—
3.74(3)	61.	3.23 (2)	20.	4.28(2)	21.	10.87(4)	113.
17.58 (2)	62.	19.00(3)	50.	13.48(2)	45.	14.98(2)	42.
1.25	20.3	1.62	10.	2.14	10.5	2.72	28.2
6.74	22.5	7.49	21.	8.09	18.7	8.79	31.
1.37	17.	1.62	18.	2.21	15.	2.63	58.
1.16 1.33	3. 16.	—	—	—	—	3.00 2.54 2.59	13. 50. 4.
1.30 1.37	2. 68.	1.92	6.	—	—	2.98 2.91	41. 9.
6.53 (5)	106.0	3.54 (2)	24.	2.21 (1)	15.	16.65(6)	175.
6.93 (1)	38.	14.36(2)	90.	7.92 (1)	43.	16.51(2)	94.
		1.77	12.	2.21	15.	2.77	29.2
6.93	38.	7.18	45.	7.92	43.	8.26	47.

4.83	11.	5.24	17.7	5.76
—	—	—	—	—
4.75	71.	5.30	10.	5.78
4.63	81.	5.29	37.	5.75
9.38 (2)	152.	10.59 (2)	47.	11.53 (
4.69	76.	5.29	23.5	5.76
—	—	5.18	12.	—

1.45	30	—	—	2.36 2.06	11. 10.	2.82	31.
—	—	1.90	19.	2.49	6.	2.77 2.64	2. 30.
—	—	1.93 1.83	13. 4.	—	—	2.59 2.67	2. 40.
1.45 (1)	30.	5.66 (3)	36.	6.91 (3)	27.	13.49 (5)	105.
1.45	30.	1.89	12.	2.30	9.	2.70	21.
1.12	78.	1.61 1.99 1.88	25. 30. 20.	—	—	2.80	66.
1.06	74.	1.63 1.88	16. 30.	2.21	5.	—	—
1.42 1.07	18. 64.	1.98	32.	2.11	5.	—	—
4.67 (4)	234.	10.97 (6)	153.	4.32 (2)	10.	2.80 (1)	66.
6.64 (1)	32.	4.24 (2)	70.	26.06 (3)	241.		
1.17	58.5	1.83	25.5	2.16	5.	2.80	66.
6.64	32.	7.12	35.	8.69	80.3		
—	—	1.70 1.88	75. 65.	—	—	2.71 2.75	42. 67.
—	—	1.88 1.69 1.85	100. 68. 22.	—	—	2.88 2.86 2.78	60. 48. 94.
—	—	1.99 1.58	97. 106.	—	—	2.75 2.57	55. 26.
—	—	12.57 (7)	533.	—	—	19.30 (7)	392.
13.18 (2)	81.						

4.41 4.13	58. 37.	4.50	34.	5.23	22.
4.38 4.08	60. 57.	4.67	55.	5.16 5.03	35. 35.
21.22 (5)	255.	13.89 (3)	133.	20.70 (4)	124
4.24	51.	4.63	44.3	5.18	31.
4.37 4.37	66. 63.	4.74 4.81	61. 58.	—	—
4.19 4.14	72 55.	4.84	67.	—	—
4.35	80.	4.60 4.64	77. 88.	5.09	84.
21.42 (5)	336.	23.63 (5)	351.	5.09 (1)	84.
4.28	67.2	4.73	70.2	5.09	84.
55"– R.	60" P.	60"– R.	66" P.	66"– R.	70" P.
55.33 (1)	71.91	129.23 (2)	106.85	68.01 (1)	62.3
55.33	71.91	64.62	53.43	68.01	62.3

5.10 (3)	480.8	
1.70 (1)	160.3	—
1.67	112.0	2.35 2.09 4.44 (
1.67	112.0	2.22 (
1.99	158.8	2.30 2.45

—	—	5.74 (
5.29	17.4	5.73
		5.72
		5.64
		17.09 (
5.29	17.4	5.70 (
5.07	14.2	5.98
5.27	9.7	5.95
5.46	12.8	5.65
5.05	14.8	17.58 (
20.85 (4)	51.5	
5.21 (4)	12.9	5.86 (
5.10	9.8	5.99
5.24	16.0	5.73
		5.83
10.34 (2)	25.8	5.61

1.62 (3)	99.5	2.42 (2)	35.6
40" –	42"	42" –	43"
R.	P.	R.	P.
81.42	108.0	42.37	63.0
(2)		(1)	
22.04"		26.85"	
40.71	54.0	42.37	63.0

… of Monthly Aver…

Jan.	Feb.	Mar.	April
4.33"	4.15	3.97	3.36
2.82"	3.33	4.02	3.40
65.1%	80.2	101.3	101.2

[illegible] (3)	[illegible]	—	—
—	—	5.34	71.3
—	—	5.34	71.3
53"–	56"	61"–	64"
R.	P	R.	P
325.72	317.0	125.19	106.0
(6)		(2)	
28.77"		33.05"	
54.29	52.8	62.60	53.0

1.78	161.4	2.37
1.82	82.1	2.00
1.85	126.3	2.22
1.57	164.3	2.43
5.24 (3)	372.7	6.65
1.75	124.2	2.22
1.58	125.8	2.01
1.84	50.0	2.02
3.42 (2)	175.8	4.03
1.71	87.9	2.02
1.66	54.9	2.04
		2.43
		2.14
		2.40
		2.03
		2.38

R = depth of Rainfall in inches;
P = percent. of (R) collected in stream.

3.5" — 4.0"		4.0" — 4.5"		4.5" — 5.0"		5.0" — 5.5"		5.5" — 6.0"		Over
R	P	R	P	R	P	R	P	R	P	R
3.57	56.0	4.15	45.3	4.71	46.8	5.09	34.9	5.63	57.3	6.36
		4.09	30.2			5.20	88.8	5.55	13.3	7.02
		4.06	45.4			5.37	92.4	5.95	37.2	
		4.01	37.6			15.66 (3)	216.1	5.85	57.0	
		16.31 (4)	158.5					22.98 (4)	164.8	6.36(
3.57	56.0	4.08	39.6	4.71	46.8	5.22	72.0	5.75	41.2	7.02(
3.56	77.4	4.21	54.2	4.65	53.6	5.23	107.3	5.97	66.5	6.54
3.98	74.9			4.55	85.2					6.28
3.86	43.0			4.78	95.3					8.19
3.86	56.4			13.98 (3)	234.1					7.18
3.68	48.3									
3.51	70.3									6.41(

31.5 74.7	1.79 1.81 3.60 (2)	19.9 19.5 39.4	2.20	25.1	2.68 2.65 2.67 8.00 (3)	13.2 11.4 23.8 48.4
31.5	1.80 (2)	19.7	2.20	25.1	2.67 (3)	16.1
76.9	—	—	2.30 2.13 4.43 (2)	24.5 55.1 79.6	2.83 2.72 5.55 (2)	11.0 77.0 88.0
76.9	—	—	2.22 (2)	39.8	2.78 (2)	44.0
34"	38" —	40"	41" —	44"	44" —	47"
P	R.	P	R.	P	R.	P.
34.1%	117.32 (3)	118.5	213.22 (5)	233.8	225.94 (5)	244.0
34.1%	39.11	39.5	42.64	46.8	45.19	48.8

mary of Monthly Averages for

	Jan.	Feb.	Mar.	Apr.	May	June
R=	4.23"	4.22	4.38	3.24	3.42	2.97
} C=	2.12"	3.00	5.10	3.46	1.97	0.85
} P=	49.3%	77.1	129.9	114.7	68.4	29.8

12.1	5.60	5.9
—	5.76	32.6
	5.80	42.2
	5.80	20.7
	17.36 (3)	95.5
—	5.79 (3)	31.8
31.9	—	—
100.6		
335		
54.3		
1220.3		

							14.19 (5)	252.4	3.46
									19.66 (6
84.0	~~1.23~~ omit	~~41.5~~	1.98	34.0	2.07	25.8	2.95	22.0	3.33
37.0	1.21	35.5	1.60	31.6			2.95	54.0	3.17
19.1			1.87	33.1			2.64	34.8	3.23
40.1			1.81	3.7			2.96	14.4	3.12
			1.78	79.1			2.58	47.3	3.04
			1.61	27.9			2.75	27.2	15.89 (
			10.65 (6)	209.4			16.83 (6)	199.7	
—	1.06	39.0	~~1.73~~ omit	~~0.0~~	2.16	21.0	2.63	28.0	3.10
			1.67	28.1	2.20	19.6	2.77	23.3	3.10
					2.31	14.2	2.78	5.8	3.16
					2.40	15.9	2.88	0.6	3.47
					2.22	16.9	2.99	16.7	3.38
					11.29 (5)	87.6	14.05 (5)	74.4	3.49
									3.30
									3.47
									26.47 (8

R = depth of Rainfall in inches;
P = percent. of (R) collected in lake.

3.5" – 4.0		4.0" – 4.5"		4.5" – 5.0"		5.0" – 5.5"		5.5" – 6.0"		Over 6.0"	
R	P	R	P	R	P	R	P	R	P	R	P
3.70 3.71 3.95 3.93 15.29 (4)	33.0 49.0 32.3 40.1 154.4	4.10 4.24 4.39 4.13 4.23 21.09 (5)	47.0 72.9 41.8 27.5 38.7 227.9	4.99 4.78 9.77 (2)	43.0 66.6 109.6	5.25 5.29 5.46 16.00 (3)	36.1 60.2 82.5 178.8	5.77 5.56 5.93 17.26 (3)	56.3 21.5 31.0 108.8	7.85 6.53 6.67 13.20 (2) 7.85 (1)	60.0 36.6 93.8 130.4 60.0
3.96 3.59 3.98 3.55 3.89 18.97 (5)	75.9 44.3 50.2 78.0 43.5 291.9	4.38 4.45 4.21 4.43 17.47 (4)	71.0 39.0 42.4 50.3 202.7	4.68	84.0	5.40 5.05 5.34 5.02 20.81 (4)	97.0 55.3 80.8 131.9 365.0	5.80 5.93 11.73 (2)	49.0 66.9 115.9	7.07 6.64 6.86 7.26 6.70 27.89 (4)	26.0 47.4 107.3 35.1 55.0 223.4
3.57 3.92 3.98 3.74 3.90 3.60 22.71 (6)	104.0 45.0 97.8 71.2 84.5 89.4 491.9	4.20 4.50 4.12 12.82 (3)	128.6 103.9 75.7 308.2	4.79	118.1	5.48 5.02 5.10 5.49 5.20 27.29 (5)	85.0 50.4 72.0 146.3 106.2 459.9	5.65 5.60 11.25 (2)	62.0 85.0 147.0	8.44 7.52 6.04 7.43 7.79 7.35 30.09 (4)	48.0 44.0 56.0 69.9 87.4 79.9 281.2
3.80 3.71 3.62 11.13 (3)	105.1 63.6 119.1 287.8	4.02 4.45 8.47 (2)	66.0 81.3 147.3	4.69	95.6	5.03	66.5	5.61 5.63 11.24 (2)	62.0 50.7 112.7	11.34 8.81 6.36	39.0 78.0 50.2
3.56 3.73 3.95 3.64 3.70 18.58 (5)	39.9 54.6 31.9 32.9 24.6 183.9	4.25	32.8	4.73 4.63 9.36 (2)	32.8 57.2 84.0	5.31 5.46 5.45 16.22 (3)	34.9 37.1 33.5 105.5	5.66	35.3	8.25 6.46 6.46 8.12 7.59 12.92 (2) 16.37 (2)	57.0 20.0 34.0 76.0 29.0 54.0 133.0
3.68 3.88 3.78 11.34 (3)	29.0 17.3 20.4 66.7	4.05 4.27 4.14 4.28 16.74 (4)	24.0 34.8 18.6 27.8 105.2	4.80 4.79 4.83 14.42 (3)	23.0 40.8 27.0 90.8	—	—	5.96	14.6	6.24	23.7
3.57 3.77 3.61 10.95 (3)	7.1 13.2 10.4 30.7	4.08 4.42 8.50 (2)	15.1 5.0 20.1	4.71 4.80 9.51 (2)	11.8 15.7 27.5	5.36	11.0	5.55	2.6	14.12 13.35 9.49 7.00 9.10 18.59 (2) 27.47 (2)	21.0 9.0 8.9 4.7 17.9 26.8 30.0

120.0	1.70	48.9	2.05 2.06 2.33 2.08 8.52 (

5.38	12.8
5.15	14.3
5.16	11.5
5.26	15.0
5.14	12.8
26.09 (5)	66.4
5.45	23.0
5.26	39.0
5.14	21.2
15.85 (3)	83.2

174.5 280.1 454.6	—	—	2.49 2.49 2.22 2.29 9.49 (4)	78.4 168.4 84.8 70.2 401.8	2.55	177.3	3.00 3.30 6.30 (2)	105.2 104.7 209.9
—	1.54 1.78 3.32 (2)	141.1 183.5 324.6	2.18 2.11 2.47 2.10 2.41 11.27 (5)	68.8 55.0 65.9 154.3 121.8 465.8	2.84 2.86 5.70 (2)	115.2 75.1 190.3	3.18 3.45 3.15 3.37 3.48 16.63 (5)	121.2 58.8 109.0 80.7 65.4 435.1
—	1.86 1.69 3.55 (2)	104.9 112.0 216.9	2.02 2.46 2.01 6.49 (3)	47.3 57.0 38.5 142.8	2.98 2.95 2.95 8.88 (3)	50.7 50.2 43.0 143.9	3.15	36.0
34.3	1.64 1.54 3.18 (2)	31.8 35.5 67.3	2.09 2.20 2.10 2.35 8.74 (4)	38.6 38.1 49.5 31.9 158.1	2.62 2.70 5.32 (2)	29.6 47.3 76.9	3.32 3.38 6.70 (2)	57.0 56.9 113.9
—	—	—	2.39 2.34 2.04 2.23 2.27 2.04 2.42 15.73 (7)	22.6 14.9 22.8 17.5 19.0 23.2 16.2 136.2	2.60 2.79 2.58 7.97 (3)	33.3 10.8 25.7 69.8	3.18 3.45 6.63 (2)	13.3 14.2 27.5
20.8	—	—	—	—	2.52 2.61 5.13 (2)	15.1 12.9 28.0	3.24 3.44 6.68 (2)	7.8 27.6 35.4

R = depth of Rainfall in inches;
P = percent of (R) collected in lake.

4.5"–5.0"		5.0"–5.5"		5.5"–6.0"		Over 6.0"	
R	P	R	P	R	P	R	P
4.75	31.5	5.25	60.2	5.67	62.6	6.32	36.6
4.83	37.1			5.82	14.2	6.25	100.7
4.52	55.0			5.55	24.8	12.57 (2)	137.3
14.10 (3)	123.6			5.51	81.8		
				22.55 (4)	183.4		
4.68	64.8	5.08	117.6	5.74	69.2	6.09	63.9
		5.09	66.8			7.18	107.3
		10.17 (2)	184.4			7.50	28.6
						6.09 (1)	63.9
						14.68 (2)	135.9

		31" – 34"		34"
		R.	P	R.
Yearly	Totals	31.22"	29.8%	69.72
	No.	(1)		(
Yearly	Means	31.22"	29.8%	34.86

Average Rainfall in inches

" depth of Rain collected in

" percentage " " "

5.45	7.2	5.52 5.58 11.10 (2)	12.2 10.5 22.7	8.84 10.20	29.5 14.4	3.98" 24.9%
—	—	5.69 5.65 11.34 (2)	30.8 44.1 74.9	6.31 ~~6.85~~ 7.26 6.32 12.63 (2)	38.2 ~~73.6~~ 37.8 16.2 54.4	3.79" 33.8% 7.26 / 37.8 (1)
5.27	96.4	—	—	—	—	3.47" 49.0%
Totals. 43.82" 19.85" 44.60%						

—	—	9.76 (1)	69.3				
—	—	—	—				
7.85 (1)	60.0	—	—				
—	—	—	—				
7.85 (1)	60.0	9.76 (1)	69.3				
7.85	60.0	9.76	69.3				
5.47 (3)	236.0	2.37 (1)	64.0	2.90 (1)	100.0	6.31 (2)	173.0
—	—	2.33 (1)	99.6	8.55 (3)	296.1	6.56 (2)	171.1
1.65 (1)	116.4	—	—	2.91 (1)	59.0	6.29 (2)	126.6
3.26 (2)	162.9	4.73 (2)	163.8	8.56 (3)	191.8	9.41 (3)	232.5
1.86 (1)	98.2	2.49 (1)	56.1	2.73 (1)	85.4	19.46 (6)	382.3
12.24 (7)	613.5	11.92 (5)	383.5	25.65 (9)	732.3	48.03 (15)	1085.5
1.75	87.6	2.38	76.7	2.85	81.4	3.20	72.4
7.5 — 8.0		8.0 — 8.5					
15.69 (2)	119.0	—	—				
—	—	—	—				
—	—	8.19 (1)	30.3				
—	—	—	—				
—	—	—	—				
15.69 (2)	119.0	8.19 (1)	30.3				
7.85	59.5	8.19	30.3				

53.9	4.23	62.9	4.70	62.0	5.25	81.4	5.70	49.8	6.28	75.7
343.0	29.75 (7)	588.0	23.68 (5)	180.0	21.05 (4)	476.0	28.70 (5)	406.0	12.19 (2)	259.0
163.2	—	—	19.11 (4)	257.7	25.77 (5)	384.6	5.96 (1)	70.0	24.74 (4)	319.0
451.1	4.21 (1)	54.2	13.98 (3)	234.1	5.23 (1)	107.3	5.97 (1)	66.5	12.82 (2)	195.7
291.9	17.47 (4)	202.7	4.68 (1)	84.0	20.81 (4)	365.0	11.73 (2)	115.9	6.04 (1)	77.4
58.9	8.70 (2)	140.9	4.68 (1)	64.8	10.17 (2)	184.4	5.74 (1)	69.2	6.09 (1)	63.9
1308.1	60.13 (14)	985.8	66.13 (14)	1120.6	83.03 (16)	1517.3	58.10 (10)	727.6	61.88 (10)	885.0
72.7	4.30	70.4	4.72	80.0	5.19	94.8	5.81	72.8	6.19	88.5

March.

P.N.T.	—	—	3.81 (3)	533.0	4.83 (3)	543.0	9.52 (4)	428.0	11.51 (4)	578.0
Cr.	—	—	1.29 (1)	156.6	5.10 (3)	480.8	—	—	5.49 (2)	133.0
Sud.	—	—	2.51 (2)	540.3	1.78 (1)	161.4	2.37 (1)	100.9	5.63 (2)	335.4
Co.	—	—	3.44 (3)	577.1	1.76 (1)	115.8	2.28 (1)	91.5	8.10 (3)	349.3
M.	—	—	2.27 (2)	454.6	—	—	9.49 (4)	401.8	2.55 (1)	177.3
Totals	—	—	13.32 (11)	2261.6	13.47 (8)	1301.0	23.66 (10)	1022.2	33.28 (12)	1573.0
Av'ge	—	—	1.21	205.6	1.68	162.6	2.37	102.2	2.77	131.1

March, Continued.

	6.5 – 7.0		7.5 – 8.0		8.0 – 8.5	
P.N.T.	13.33 (2)	179.0	—	—	—	—
Cr.	—	—	7.66 (1)	90.0	—	—
Sud.	—	—	15.16 (2)	190.6	8.36 (1)	102.7
Co.	—	—	30.09 (4)	281.2	8.44 (1)	48.0
M.	13.37 (2)	181.9	—	—	—	—
Totals	26.70 (4)	360.9	52.91 (7)	561.8	16.80 (2)	150.7
Av'ge	6.67	90.2	7.56	80.3	8.40	75.3

April.

P.N.T.	—	—	1.48 (1)	50.0	13.07 (7)	473.0	14.26 (6)	443.0	19.24 (7)	627.0
Cr.	—	—	2.44 (2)	228.8	1.67 (1)	112.0	4.44 (2)	251.1	8.44 (3)	337.6
Sud.	0.83 (1)	181.1	—	—	5.24 (3)	372.7	6.65 (3)	472.8	5.47 (2)	215.0
Co.	0.78 (1)	115.5	—	—	10.88 (6)	695.5	9.17 (4)	383.9	13.31 (5)	443.0
M.	0.82 (1)	163.6	—	—	3.32 (2)	324.6	11.27 (5)	465.8	5.70 (2)	190.3
Totals	2.43 (3)	460.2	3.92 (3)	278.8	34.18 (19)	1977.8	45.75 (20)	2016.6	52.21 (19)	1812.9
Av'ge	0.81	153.4	1.31	92.9	1.80	104.1	2.29	100.8	2.75	95.4

April, Continued.

	8.5 – 9.0		11.0 – 11.5	
P.N.T.	—	—	—	—
Cr.	—	—	—	—
Sud.	—	—	—	—
Co.	8.81 (1)	78.0	11.34 (1)	39.0
M.	—	—	—	—
Totals	8.81 (1)	78.0	11.34 (1)	39.0
Av'ge	8.81	78.0	11.34	39.0

4.21	96.9	4.77	102.7	5.28	96.1	5.66	88.5	6.20	93.8
8.19 (2)	161.0	19.66 (4)	224.0	15.87 (3)	188.0	—	—	6.12 (1)	57.0
8.85 (2)	199.9	—	—	10.55 (2)	173.3	—	—	6.31 (1)	56.7
12.88 (3)	353.2	4.72 (1)	114.1	5.25 (1)	82.7	5.79 (1)	48.5	—	—
8.47 (2)	147.3	4.69 (1)	95.6	5.03 (1)	66.5	11.24 (2)	112.7	6.36 (1)	50.2
4.19 (1)	70.6	9.26 (2)	166.6	—	—	5.73 (1)	38.6	—	—
42.58 (10)	932.0	38.33 (8)	650.3	36.70 (7)	510.5	22.76 (4)	199.8	18.79 (3)	163.9
4.26	93.2	4.79	75.0	5.24	72.9	5.69	50.0	6.26	54.6

—	—	—	—	3.84 (2)	72.0	9.24
0.85 (1)	103.5	3.61 (3)	317.0	1.99 (1)	158.8	7.19
0.96 (1)	260.2	1.17 (1)	154.5	3.42 (2)	175.8	4.03
0.83 (1)	200.0	2.22 (2)	229.0	3.65 (2)	75.0	4.30
0.67 (1)	322.9	—	—	3.55 (2)	216.9	6.49
3.31 (4)	886.6	7.00 (6)	700.5	16.45 (9)	698.5	31.25
0.83	221.7	1.17	116.8	1.83	77.6	2.23

May, Continued.

6.5 — 7.0		7.0 — 7.5		7.5 — 8.0		8.0
—	—	7.14 (1)	48.0	7.62 (1)	36.0	—
—	—	—	—	—	—	8.16
6.61 (1)	77.8	—	—	—	—	—
—	—	—	—	7.59 (1)	29.0	16.37
—	—	—	—	—	—	—
6.61 (1)	77.8	7.14 (1)	48.0	15.21 (2)	65.0	24.55
6.61	77.8	7.14	48.0	7.61	32.5	8.18

June.

0.84 (1)	9.0	1.48 (1)	19.0	4.99 (3)	38.0	4.74
0.71 (1)	76.0	2.47 (2)	89.4	3.50 (2)	128.4	8.53
—	—	2.63 (2)	86.5	1.66 (1)	54.9	13.42
1.87 (3)	240.1	1.21 (1)	35.5	10.65 (6)	209.4	2.07
0.72 (1)	125.8	1.49 (1)	34.3	3.18 (2)	67.3	8.74
4.14 (6)	450.9	9.28 (7)	264.7	23.98 (14)	498.0	37.50
0.69	75.2	1.33	37.8	1.71	35.6	2.21

June, Continued.

44.3	5.28	39.7	5.68	35.1
77.0	20.82 (4)	138.0	17.31 (3)	50.0
75.7	5.29 (1)	17.4	17.09 (3)	64.3
—	5.40 (1)	42.8	—	—
90.8	—	—	5.96 (1)	14.6
18.3	—	—	5.69 (1)	38.5
261.8	31.51 (6)	198.2	46.05 (8)	167.4
23.8	5.25	33.0	5.76	20.9

14.54 (2)	51.0	15.52 (2)	31.0	32.81 (4)	107.0
—	—	7.74 (1)	20.7	—	—
—	—	—	—	—	—
7.00 (1)	4.7	—	—	—	—
7.23 (1)	9.2	—	—	8.46 (1)	15.8
28.77 (4)	64.9	23.26 (3)	51.7	41.27 (5)	122.[illegible]
7.19	16.2	7.75	17.2	8.25	24.6

3.74 (3)	61.0	3.23 (2)	20.0	4.28 (2)	21.0
2.65 (2)	102.4	1.71 (1)	30.4	2.09 (1)	24.9
1.36 (1)	19.4	3.39 (2)	47.9	4.43 (2)	22.7
2.27 (2)	13.8	—	—	8.99 (4)	77.7
1.07 (1)	20.8	—	—	—	—
11.09 (9)	217.4	8.33 (5)	98.3	19.79 (9)	146.3
1.23	24.2	1.67	19.7	2.20	16.3

ontinued.

7.0 — 7.5		8.0 — 8.5		8.5 — 9.0	
14.98 (2)	45.0	24.26 (3)	56.0	17.58 (2)	62.0
28.34 (4)	85.2	—	—	—	—
14.13 (2)	18.2	—	—	—	—
28.50 (4)	52.3	—	—	—	—
7.51 (1)	14.8	—	—	—	—
93.46 (13)	215.5	24.26 (3)	56.0	17.58 (2)	62.0
7.19	16.6	8.09	18.7	8.79	31.0

Dec. 1, 1896.

Summary of Average Rainfalls and Corresponding Run-offs (R) and (F) with Number of Occurrences, during the several months, on the Watersheds of Croton River, 1870-94; Sudbury River, 1875-1897; Cochituate Lake 1863-1897; Mystic Lake, 1878-97; Perkiomen, Neshaminy & Tohickon Creeks 1884-1897. ([illegible])

		0.0" to 1.0"	1.0" to 1.5"	1.5" to 2.0"	2.0" to 2.5"	2.5" to 3.0"	3.0" to 3.5"	3.5" to 4.0"	4.0" to 4.5"	4.5" to 5.0"	5.0" to 5.5"	5.5" to 6.0"	6.0" to 6.5"	6.5" to 7.0"	7.0" to 7.5"	7.5" to 8.0"	8.0" to 8.5"	8.5" to 9.0"	9.0" to 10.0"	10.0" to 11.0"	11.0" to 12.0"	over 12"
Jan.	No.	1	6	8	14	17	7	14	21	10	17	16	6	3	1	1	—	—	1	—	—	—
	R	0.91"	1.35	1.83	2.28	2.75	3.24	3.79	4.23	4.70	5.25	5.70	6.28	6.72	7.02	7.85	—	—	9.76	—	—	—
	F	65.0%	78.8	55.1	61.5	52.1	50.8	53.9	62.9	62.0	81.4	49.8	75.7	82.3	76.7	60.0	—	—	69.3	—	—	—
Feb.	No.	6	9	7	5	9	15	18	14	14	16	10	10	4	3	2	1	—	—	—	—	—
	R	0.78	1.23	1.75	2.38	2.85	3.20	3.79	4.30	4.72	5.19	5.81	6.19	6.97	7.29	7.85	8.17	—	—	—	—	—
	F	187.7	98.1	87.6	76.7	81.4	72.4	72.7	70.4	80.0	94.8	72.8	88.5	55.8	66.0	59.5	30.3	—	—	—	—	—
Mar.	No.	—	11	8	10	12	15	20	14	15	16	4	8	4	—	7	2	—	—	—	—	—
	R	—	1.21	1.68	2.37	2.77	3.19	3.74	4.21	4.77	5.28	5.66	6.20	6.67	—	7.56	8.40	—	—	—	—	—
	F	—	205.6	162.6	102.2	131.1	111.3	92.7	96.9	102.7	96.1	88.5	93.8	90.2	—	80.3	75.3	—	—	—	—	—
Apr.	No.	3	3	19	20	19	30	14	10	8	7	4	3	—	—	—	—	1	—	—	1	—
	R	0.81	1.31	1.80	2.29	2.75	3.24	3.74	4.26	4.79	5.24	5.69	6.26	—	—	—	—	8.81	—	—	11.34	—
	F	153.4	92.9	104.1	100.8	95.4	90.4	96.5	93.2	75.0	72.9	50.0	54.6	—	—	—	—	78.0	—	—	39.0	—
May	No.	4	6	9	14	21	15	15	6	11	11	8	10	1	1	2	3	2	—	—	1	2
	R	0.83	1.17	1.83	2.23	2.84	3.28	3.70	4.23	4.75	5.28	5.68	6.40	6.62	7.14	7.61	8.12	8.81	—	—	11.64	12.57
	F	221.7	116.8	77.6	46.6	40.5	46.0	40.0	43.7	44.3	39.7	35.1	41.5	77.8	48.0	32.5	68.7	48.5	—	—	57.0	60.0
June	No.	6	7	14	17	18	20	14	13	11	6	8	3	1	3	1	—	—	—	—	—	—
	R	0.69	1.33	1.71	2.21	2.73	3.22	3.74	4.24	4.68	5.25	5.76	6.32	6.84	7.12	7.70	—	—	—	—	—	—
	F	75.2	37.8	35.6	34.7	30.4	25.1	22.5	21.8	23.8	33.0	20.9	33.6	29.9	31.0	14.8	—	—	—	—	—	—
July	No.	—	3	4	24	16	18	16	10	4	18	6	1	2	4	3	5	1	6	—	—	6
	R	—	1.30	1.70	2.26	2.77	3.30	3.70	4.31	4.75	5.24	5.78	6.37	6.57	7.19	7.75	8.25	8.63	9.12	—	—	12.96
	F	—	20.6	19.5	16.8	16.0	12.2	13.0	12.6	12.3	15.3	11.4	5.0	12.7	16.2	17.2	24.6	24.0	16.2	—	—	30.9
Aug.	No.	4	7	5	9	10	11	22	6	11	9	11	9	2	13	—	3	2	1	1	—	1
	R	0.75	1.23	1.67	2.20	2.65	3.34	3.78	4.27	4.76	5.33	5.74	6.32	6.74	7.19	—	8.09	8.77	9.76	10.38	—	12.36
	F	22.1	24.2	19.7	16.3	23.4	16.9	17.0	8.7	26.4	14.0	15.9	13.8	22.5	16.6	—	18.7	21.0	13.5	52.5	—	17.0
Sept.	No.	14	9	17	15	21	11	7	1	4	2	3	4	3	2	2	11	2	2	1	—	1
	R	0.70	1.32	1.68	2.18	2.75	3.30	3.72	4.06	4.71	5.20	5.90	6.31	6.80	7.28	7.82	8.37	8.67	9.00	10.77	—	14.33
	F	33.4	25.8	22.5	22.1	20.6	18.5	21.9	10.0	24.2	9.6	19.4	27.8	33.0	13.0	25.9	21.0	18.6	38.0	28.6	—	22.4
Oct.	No.	10	5	7	13	12	13	19	6	15	14	5	8	1	2	1	3	2	3	3	—	—
	R	0.72	1.25	1.85	2.27	2.76	3.25	3.71	4.10	4.79	5.24	5.64	6.28	6.99	7.13	7.63	8.16	8.68	9.73	10.46	—	—
	F	40.0	43.9	20.0	22.0	16.2	22.3	21.7	22.5	31.6	21.2	8.7	29.5	9.3	12.0	43.4	12.8	21.4	26.4	25.3	—	—
Nov.	No.	1	8	14	10	15	14	10	14	14	7	8	9	9	3	—	3	4	—	—	—	—
	R	0.93	1.20	1.81	2.18	2.75	3.26	3.71	4.29	4.68	5.22	5.76	6.30	6.87	7.37	—	8.15	8.65	—	—	—	—
	F	62.4	88.8	28.8	24.0	28.2	44.9	31.4	46.8	34.4	29.6	34.1	34.2	42.9	35.9	—	42.9	68.0	—	—	—	—
Dec.	No.	5	5	12	10	17	17	18	15	13	12	4	5	4	1	—	—	1	—	—	—	—
	R	0.86	1.21	1.75	2.28	2.73	3.24	3.76	4.30	4.77	5.21	5.78	6.19	6.61	7.34	—	—	8.74	—	—	—	—
	F	107.9	76.5	76.7	49.5	59.9	50.9	37.2	49.1	57.7	58.5	47.0	68.8	35.9	52.7	—	—	86.6	—	—	—	—

8.0	9.38 (2)	152.0	10.59 (2)	47.0	11.53 (2)	27.0	19.00 (3)	50.0
—	9.20 (2)	38.5	10.34 (2)	25.8	23.16 (4)	74.5	6.12 (1)	14.4
30.6	9.38 (2)	15.9	10.70 (2)	13.1	5.53 (1)	12.8	12.74 (2)	21.7
13.6	9.74 (2)	33.8	—	—	17.00 (3)	51.4	12.75 (2)	29.6
—	14.65 (3)	49.7	16.33 (3)	40.1	5.90 (1)	9.2	6.23 (1)	8.8
52.2	52.35 (11)	289.9	47.96 (9)	126.0	63.12 (11)	174.9	56.84 (9)	124.5
8.7	4.76	26.4	5.33	14.0	5.74	15.9	6.32	13.8

0.70	33.4	1.33	25.8	1.68	22.5	2.18	22.1	2.75

September, Continued.

6.5 — 7.0		7.0 — 7.5		7.5 — 8.0		8.0 — 8.5		8.5–
6.93 (1)	38.0	14.36 (2)	90.0	7.92 (1)	43.0	16.51 (2)	94.0	—
13.47 (2)	61.1	7.49 (1)	9.2	—	—	—	—	—
—	—	—	—	7.72 (1)	8.7	—	—	17.33 (
—	—	—	—	—	—	50.76 (6)	102.2	—
—	—	—	—	—	—	24.80 (3)	35.1	—
20.40 (3)	99.1	21.85 (3)	99.2	15.64 (2)	51.7	92.07 (11)	231.3	17.33 (
6.80	33.0	7.28	33.0	7.82	25.9	8.37	21.0	8.67

October.

1.52 (3)	67.0	1.45 (1)	30.0	5.66 (3)	36.0	6.91 (3)	27.0	13.49 (
1.87 (2)	122.7	—	—	1.50 (1)	25.3	8.98 (4)	138.5	—
1.28 (2)	51.3	1.17 (1)	19.2	—	—	6.79 (3)	50.3	5.80 (
1.79 (2)	115.1	3.65 (3)	170.5	2.00 (1)	24.3	4.71 (2)	56.6	5.54 (
0.77 (1)	44.2	—	—	3.78 (2)	54.3	2.16 (1)	13.6	8.25 (
7.23 (10)	400.3	6.27 (5)	219.7	12.94 (7)	139.9	29.55 (13)	286.0	33.08 (
0.72	40.0	1.25	43.9	1.85	20.0	2.27	22.0	2.76

October, Continued.

6.5 — 7.0		7.0 — 7.5		7.5 — 8.0		8.0 — 8.5		8.5–
—	—	—	—	—	—	—	—	—
6.99 (1)	9.3	—	—	7.63 (1)	43.4	8.38 (1)	13.2	—
—	—	—	—	—	—	—	—	8.52 (
—	—	14.26 (2)	24.0	—	—	16.10 (2)	28.3	—
—	—	—	—	—	—	—	—	8.84 (
6.99 (1)	9.3	14.26 (2)	24.0	7.63 (1)	43.4	24.48 (3)	41.5	17.36 (
6.99	9.3	7.13	12.0	7.63	43.4	8.16	13.8	8.68

21.00 (4)	161.0	5.56 (1)	3.0	18.62 (3)	118.0
10.32 (2)	38.1	5.94 (1)	11.8	12.60 (2)	48.1
10.45 (2)	24.3	5.60 (1)	5.9	6.42 (1)	14.3
26.09 (5)	66.4	—	—	12.61 (2)	55.4
5.45 (1)	7.2	11.10 (2)	22.7	—	—
73.31 (14)	297.0	28.20 (5)	43.4	50.25 (8)	235.8
5.24	21.2	5.64	8.7	6.28	29.5

November

P.N.T.	—	—	4.67 (4)	234.0	10.97 (6)	153.0	4.32 (2)	10.0	2.80 (1)	66.0	16.20 (5)	334.[illegible]
Cr.	—	—	1.12 (1)	183.9	3.45 (2)	95.2	2.49 (1)	32.1	10.89 (4)	105.0	6.72 (2)	75.1
Sud.	—	—	1.15 (1)	31.5	3.60 (2)	39.4	2.20 (1)	25.1	8.00 (3)	48.4	9.54 (3)	96.8
Co.	0.93 (1)	62.4	1.24 (1)	120.0	1.70 (1)	48.9	8.52 (4)	123.5	14.21 (5)	165.3	3.26 (1)	40.0
M.	—	—	1.39 (1)	141.2	5.63 (3)	66.6	4.26 (2)	48.9	5.37 (2)	37.9	9.86 (3)	82.8
Totals	0.93 (1)	62.4	9.57 (8)	710.6	25.35 (14)	403.1	21.79 (10)	239.6	41.27 (15)	422.6	45.58 (14)	628.7
Av'ge	0.93	62.4	1.20	88.8	1.81	28.8	2.18	24.0	2.75	28.2	3.26	44.9

November, Continued.

	6.5 — 7.0		7.0 — 7.5		8.0 — 8.5		8.5 — 9.0	
P.N.T.	6.64 (1)	32.0	14.24 (2)	70.0	—	—	26.06 (3)	241.0
Cr.	—	—	—	—	24.46 (3)	128.6	—	—
Sud.	20.87 (3)	179.9	—	—	—	—	—	—
Co.	34.34 (5)	174.3	—	—	—	—	8.54 (1)	31.0
M.	—	—	7.26 (1)	37.8	—	—	—	—
Totals	61.85 (9)	386.2	21.50 (3)	107.8	24.46 (3)	128.6	34.60 (4)	272.0
Av'ge	6.87	42.9	7.17	35.9	8.15	42.9	8.65	68.0

December.

P.N.T.	2.44 (3)	299.0	—	—	12.57 (7)	533.0	—	—	19.30 (7)	392.0	15.84 (5)	331.0
Cr.	—	—	2.60 (2)	159.4	4.86 (3)	298.6	4.84 (2)	71.1	8.21 (3)	280.7	3.45 (1)	18.3
Sud.	0.94 (1)	110.7	1.13 (1)	76.9	—	—	4.43 (2)	79.6	5.55 (2)	88.0	6.49 (2)	222.2
Co.	0.94 (1)	129.8	1.18 (1)	71.1	3.60 (2)	88.9	6.64 (3)	173.6	5.27 (2)	112.4	22.60 (7)	242.[illegible]
M.	—	—	1.15 (1)	75.2	—	—	6.86 (3)	170.8	8.36 (3)	145.5	6.70 (2)	51.9
Totals	4.32 (5)	539.5	6.06 (5)	382.6	21.03 (12)	920.5	22.77 (10)	495.1	46.69 (17)	1018.6	55.08 (17)	865.9
Av'ge	0.86	107.9	1.21	76.5	1.75	76.7	2.28	49.5	2.73	59.9	3.24	50.9

December, Continued.

	6.5 — 7.0		7.0 — 7.5		8.5 — 9.0	
P.N.T.	13.18 (2)	81.0	—	—	—	—
Cr.	13.24 (2)	62.7	7.34 (1)	50.7	8.74 (1)	81.6
Sud.	—	—	—	—	—	—
Co.	—	—	—	—	—	—
M.	—	—	—	—	—	—
Totals	26.42 (4)	143.7	7.34 (1)	50.7	8.74 (1)	81.6
Av'ge	6.61	35.9	7.34	50.7	8.74	81.6

18.66 (5)	187.0	21.22 (5)	255.0	13.89 (3)	133.0	20.70 (4)	124.0	—	—	6.38 (1)	27.0
7.58 (2)	64.7	22.01 (5)	280.1	14.02 (3)	107.8	—	—	11.56 (2)	51.6	—	—
—	—	4.09 (1)	16.7	9.48 (2)	71.5	—	—	17.36 (3)	95.5	18.80 (3)	111.1
7.38 (2)	47.9	8.62 (2)	67.4	23.43 (5)	146.1	15.85 (3)	83.2	5.79 (1)	50.9	18.88 (3)	115.5
3.52 (1)	14.3	4.07 (1)	21.7	4.65 (1)	23.1	—	—	11.34 (2)	74.9	12.63 (2)	54.4
37.14 (10)	313.9	60.01 (14)	640.9	65.47 (14)	481.5	36.55 (7)	207.2	46.05 (8)	272.9	56.69 (9)	308.0
3.71	31.4	4.29	45.8	4.68	34.4	5.22	29.6	5.76	34.1	6.30	34.2

11.31 (3)	185.0	21.42 (5)	336.0	23.63 (5)	351.0	5.09 (1)	84.0	5.70 (1)	80.0	18.43 (3)	172.0
11.23 (3)	136.5	17.11 (4)	212.4	—	—	5.34 (1)	71.3	5.65 (1)	25.1	6.13 (1)	82.8
18.70 (5)	122.8	4.34 (1)	19.0	14.65 (3)	92.3	21.09 (4)	220.3	—	—	6.37 (1)	89.0
15.18 (4)	159.1	12.98 (3)	93.1	4.81 (1)	44.8	25.77 (5)	229.6	11.75 (2)	82.7	—	—
11.29 (3)	66.9	8.71 (2)	76.2	18.91 (4)	183.7	5.27 (1)	96.4	—	—	—	—
67.71 (18)	670.3	64.56 (15)	736.7	62.00 (13)	671.8	62.56 (12)	701.6	23.10 (4)	187.8	30.93 (5)	343.8
3.76	37.2	4.30	49.1	4.77	51.7	5.21	58.5	5.78	47.0	6.19	68.8

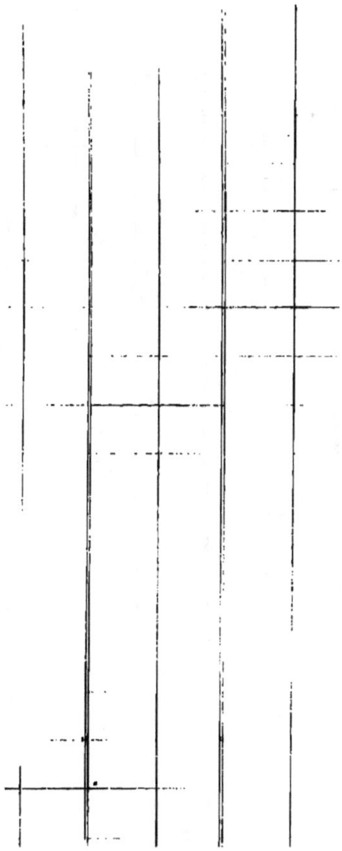

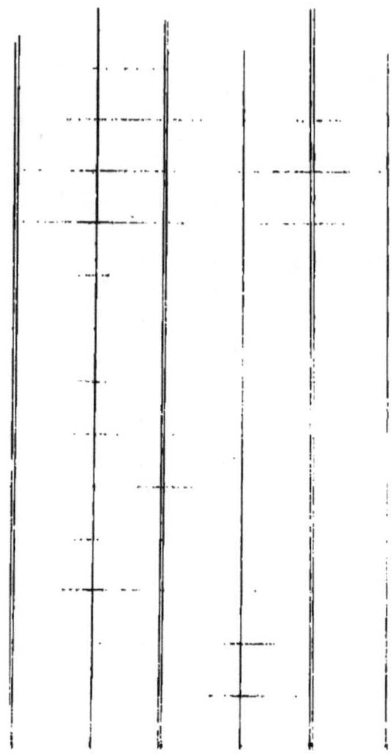

May. 1896

Reservoir at Elmira Reformatory.

May 16. 1896. Z. R. Brockway, Gen'l Supt.; David Shay. in charge of dam. Earth embankment; original max. height = 37.5′; raised 2′ twice, giving pres. max. height = 41.5′; Overflow elevation or level is 2.75′ below present ~~top~~ or crest of dam.; this has also been raised. Overflow is of masonry, & substantial. Original dam built by Mr. Beach, of Syracuse, while the two additions of 2′ each were made by Mr. Shay.

Overflow level dimensions of reservoir are as per Fig. 2, measured by Mr. Shay May 16 & 17. 1896.

Fig. 1

Fig. 2

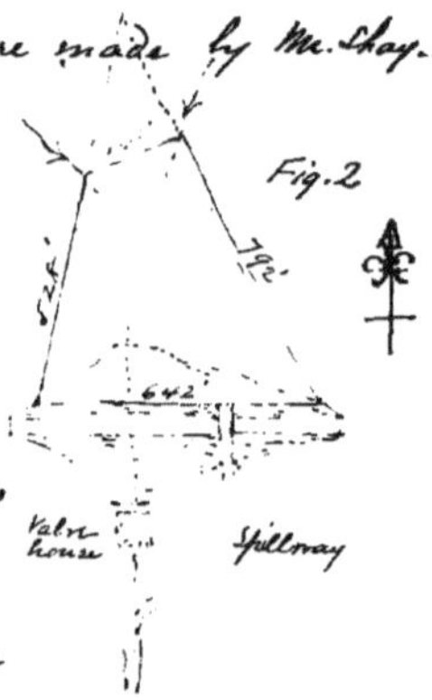

Area of full water surface = 225330 sq. ft = 5.17 acres, Given by triangles: $\left(\frac{730 \times 642}{2} - \frac{200 \times 90}{2}\right)$ (height, base; height, base).

Depth from overflow crest to top of pipe in Valve house = 38.75′; allow 3.75′ fall in pipe under bank, thus making max. depth of water = 35 ft. Call this depth 33 ft, and take volume of water as a pyramid: $V = \frac{Ah}{3} = \frac{225,300 \times 33}{3} = 2,478,300$ cft, or approx.: $V = 2,500,000$ cft $= 18,750,000$ galls.

From U. S. Survey Geolog., topogr. map, Elmira Sheet, the drainage area tributary to reservoir is 468 acres; rainfall at Elmira given = 35.5″ as per N. Y. S. Weather Bureau, 1894., average of 16 yrs. Assume Collection = 49%, or 16″; This gives on 468 acres, a volume of 27,180,000 cft/year. Deduct evaporation from water surface, average

area = 200,000 □ft and depth = 3.0', hence volume of 600000 cft/year, or say 580000 cft/year, thus leaving average available collection = 26,600,000 cft/year or 73,000 cft/day = 547,000 galls/day. In dry years may get only half.

Average number of inmates = 1400 @ 60 galls. =	84000 galls/day
1000 HP. used for 12 hrs per day, steam, @ 5 galls/HP./hr. =	60000 "
Total consumption per day — — — — — —	144,000 "

Take consumption = 150,000 galls/day and allow for 150 days drought, with no inflow except enough to balance evaporation & leakage; hence necessary storage = 22,500,000 galls, or about 4,000,000 galls. more than present max. capacity.

Raising overflow level 3 ft gives additional storage volume of 225000 × 3 = 675,000 cft = 5,062,000 galls Hence sufficient to raise said 3 ft.

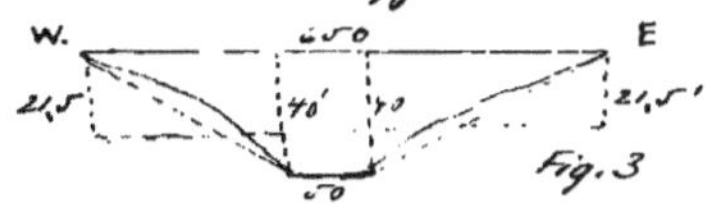

Fig. 3

The elevation of the [illegible] roughly indicated in Fig. 3, from which we find mean height = 21.5'

Volume of new embankment is:–

$\frac{37.6+14}{2} \cdot 5\frac{1}{4} \cdot 660 \times \frac{1}{27} = 3311.$ cyd

$27.6 \times 21 \times 660 \times \frac{1}{27} = 14,168.$ "

Total = 17,479 "

Fig. 4.

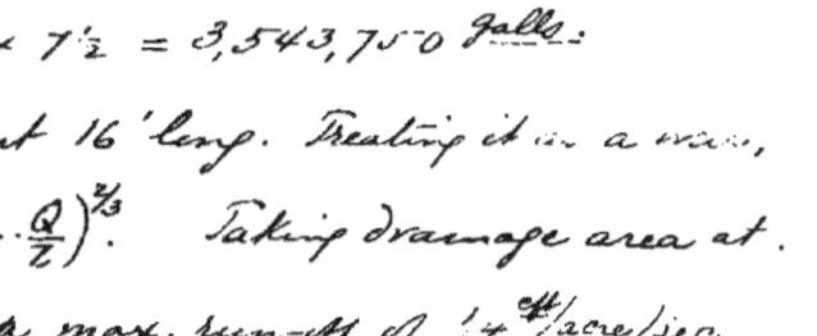

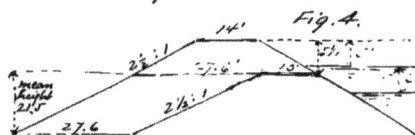

Taking this embankment as excavation from reservoir, we will increase the storage capacity: $17500 \times 27 \times 7\frac{1}{2} = 3,543,750$ galls.

The spillway overflow is about 16' long. Treating it as a weir, we will have for volume (Q): $h = \left(\frac{3}{10} \cdot \frac{Q}{l}\right)^{2/3}$. Taking drainage area at 468 acres = 0.73 □mile, and allowing a max. run-off of 1.4 cft/acre/sec., we would have $Q = \frac{468}{4} = 117$ cft/sec., say $Q = 120$ cft; hence:

$h = \left(\frac{3}{10} \cdot \frac{Q}{l}\right)^{2/3} = 1.72$ ft depth on weir, for length $l = 16$ ft.

For $Q = 90$ cft/sec., we find $h = 1.417$ ft.

Reported on May 23, 1896. Copied in Letter Book, with diagrams.

www.ingramcontent.com/pod-product-compliance
Lightning Source LLC
Chambersburg PA
CBHW030548270326
41927CB00008B/1567